AUTONOMY OF VALUES
Determinations, Affirmations And Mediations

AUTONOMY OF VALUES
Determinations, Affirmations And Mediations

Udenta O. Udenta

KRAFT BOOKS LIMITED

Published by
Kraft Books Limited
6A Polytechnic Road, Sango, Ibadan
Box 22084, University of Ibadan Post Office Ibadan,
Oyo State, Nigeria
✆ +234 (0)803 348 2474, +234 (0)805 129 1191
E-mail: kraftbooks@yahoo.com
Website: www.kraftbookslimited.com

© Udenta O. Udenta, 2015

First published 2015

ISBN 978-978-918-223-7

All Rights Reserved

Dedication

To all the guardians of the sacredness of human beings and consciousness who affirm, determine and mediate reality in its complex articulation and transformation, and particularly to: Karl Marx, Fredrich Nietzsche, Vladimir Lenin, Bertrand Russell, Ngugi Wa Thiong'o, Luciano Pavarotti, Fela Anikulapo Kuti and Michael Jackson.

Acknowledgements

Surprisingly, though **Autonomy of Values** is the most intensely personal of all my works, yet none of them can lay claim to collective ownership in the creative process in the way and manner it can. I therefore wish to thank all those who have contributed in one form or the other towards the realization of this vision; those I have shared my ideas with before even scribbling the first word; those with whom I have discussed and debated some aspects of it; and those I have virtually forced to listen as I read aloud several portions.

The list is quite long, and those whose names don't appear here must recognize that it is not that I did not value their contribution but that I cannot possibly remember all of them in over 16 or more years.

I must, first of all, thank my mentor, **Dr. Arthur Agwuncha Nwankwo** who I shared my ideas with, and who not only encouraged me to pursue it, but also ensured that his secretary, **Mr. Philip Okoye,** typed the first draft in 1997 – 1998, over and above other pressing assignments. My thanks are also due to **Prof. Gaius Igboeli** who debated aspects of the material with me, and really put me to task in clarifying my notion of value and reality. The same goes to **Hon. Ejike Nwankwo** and the late **Engr. Victor Nwankwo.**

I have also shared my ideas with my former colleagues in the Institute for Peace and Conflict Resolution, The Presidency, Abuja. To them all – the late **Prof. Osita Eze, Ambassador Ferguson Iheme, Dr. Joseph Golwa, Dr. Oshita Oshita, Dr. Ochinya Ojiji, Dr. Bakut Bakut** and **Lanre Obafemi** – I say a huge thank you. **Prof. Eze** particularly was keen to see the whole manuscript so that he will be able to do his own critique and appraisal, and most seriously warned me about the prospect of the work not seeing the light of day. The same appreciation goes to Ambassador Yusuf Mamman, a truly liberated mind whose profound intellect has been a source of constant inspiration to me in all my intellectual endeavours.

I will also mention three other people who have listened more than most to different reading sessions of the work: **Drs. Kelechi Akubueze** and **James Okoroma** and **Patrick Isiogwu.** I immensely appreciate their encouragement and support in urging me to publish the work.

I must commend my wife, **Vivian**, for her understanding, patience and love, as I spent countless hours in my study in Enugu and Abuja re-reading and re-drafting the work. She is yet to read the work, and I honestly do not know what she will make of it. I can only hope for her understanding in settling for a union with somebody who really considers himself an intellectual, in the purest expression of that term. And to my son, **Chidera,** who always dashed into my study at "critical" moments, but who would always take off when he saw that Daddy really meant business, I say a million thank you for being an understanding daddy's boy.

I will also not fail to thank my secretaries, **Kate Agama**, **Grace Ugo Thomas, Blessing........ and Lilian........** who re-typed the manuscript at different times because I had no electronic version of the hard copy **Philip Okoye** typed way back in Enugu. Their thoroughness, diligence and professional expertise in typing the work are fully appreciated.

Finally, to all the masters of consciousness whose ideas inspired and motivated me, I salute you all. Yet, it is only fitting that I add that the ideas, vision and substance of the work are wholly mine. This should even be more so given the problematic nature of some of them, which none but the author can claim responsibility for.

Preface

The universe could be quite intimidating given the range of forces and processes that define its very being, determine its fate and mediate its essence. The sheer complexity of this plethora of phenomena, mostly terrestrial, and others much less so, may suggest man's inherent inadequate apprehensible or cognitive ability in making sense out of such an infinite presence.

Yet, this need not be so. I began my quest from a very simple base: to see value, in essence, reality (other renditions of the semantic import of value that fall outside my chosen analytic and descriptive usage are irrelevant in the consideration of the work), at its most primary level. That is to say, that all forms of knowing must start at the point of production; that all productions exist autonomously at this primary level of incarnation; that affirmation and determination relate to the factor of becoming; and that in the process of becoming all value, all reality, are essentially corrupted by the element of assertion and mediation, that may take the shape of accentuation *(over-empowerment)* or attenuation *(over-disempowerment)*.

In essence, after all is said and done by man, this logic holds well with regard to politics, religion, cultural processes, technology and space probes. It held well for me in 1998 when I completed the first draft of the work. It still holds well for me, nearly a decade after, even when I have re-read and re-worked the text a thousand times over, literally speaking.

Udenta O. Udenta
Abuja, January, 2014

Content

Dedication 5
Acknowledgements 6
Preface 8
Introduction 11

Chapter One
The Production and Transformation of Values 23

Chapter Two
Cultural Reinventions: Belief, Faith and the
Immortal Instinct 38

Chapter Three
Five Life-Forms 61

Chapter Four
Ultimate Values 84

Chapter Five
Literary Values 98

Chapter Six
The Elysian Fields and the Quest for Eternal Bliss 117

Chapter Seven
Babi Yar: A Metaphor of Humanity 137

Chapter Eight
Masters of Consciousness 155

Chapter Nine
Illumination (an account of a conscious life) 185

Postscript
Reinventing Decadence: The New Culture of
Contentment – A Note 214

Afterword 221

Index 224

BY WAY OF AN INTRODUCTION

In the preface to the second edition of *Arrow of God,* Chinua Achebe, the world renowned novelist and humanist, averred that the particular attraction that novel has for him, in relation to his other novels, is that it is the work he would most likely be caught sitting down to read again. For me, the attraction of *Autonomy of Values* is that it is one work which I have re-read virtually everyday since I first finished the initial draft sometime in 1998.

In the first few weeks and months after I completed the draft, each reading session had produced an intense feeling of fulfillment, elation and surety about the realization of my objective intention. However, over the years, I have re-read the manuscript with an increasing sense of bewilderment and even embarrassment, suspicious as I have come to become, that I was reading a work written by another person. The distance between the work and myself has grown, "in leaps and bounds", as it were, to the degree that now I can no longer lay claim to a sufficient mastery of its inner meaning, theme or essence.

I have also shared reading moments with friends, beginning with *Dr. Arthur Nwankwo, Prof Gaius Igboeli, Hon. Ejike Nwankwo* and the late *Engr. Victor Nwankwo,* to listeners who are closer to me in age, and at the end of each session, I always had the sneaky feeling that while many acknowledged the beauty and flow of its language, they were as hard put as myself to make real sense out of many of its passages.

I have also pondered, with fear and trepidation, whether

it is worth the effort sharing this near surreal experience with a wider audience, and I am certain that some other writers may have also become, at one point or the other, possessed by this excruciating feeling of self-doubt. This feeling is remarkably different from the intense anticipation the publication of my first four books, starting with *Revolutionary Aesthetics and the African Literary Process,* gave me. In these works, I had waited with bated breath to see the "battle" with seen and unseen intellectual adversaries enjoy daylight and watched with pure delight as they hit the stands.

However, this feeling of self-doubt has nothing to do with an insecure intellectual position or base for, if anything, *Autonomy of Values* is a more mature work, intellectually speaking, than all my other previous works. Rather, it may well have resulted from a sense of one having embarked on a less trodden path, and most importantly by certain troubling ideas that clearly suggest that one may have crossed, like Ezeulu, the threshold of the apprehensibility of material sensations, stimuli and social responses to the acute ethereal region of occult knowledge; an Oedipal quest for transcendental consciousness, experience and reality which can wreak havoc on the secure rhythm of vital existential life-forces.

What I do recall on starting the work is that I set a task for myself, not to write an academic work but to create an unpardoned intellectual product. In so doing, I called into service, as a 34-year-old who has read fairly extensively, and who must pursue his set course from start to finish with only his ball point and plain papers before him, and with no other material to aid his cognitive and reflective abilities. That was how the work was started and finished, with no book, magazine or journal to aid the creative process, even though I have made modest references to texts and other reading materials, over the years, but only after I have "rushed through" the passages where they are relevant. The only exception to this rule was Cayley's *Classical Myths* because of the purpose it served in the writing of the chapter on "The Elysian Fields".

What defense do I have if readers present the charge that they are baffled by the apparent meaninglessness of large portions of the work; that they cannot make sense out of many of the ideas therein; and that indeed I merely played with words and language to satisfy an inner urge to say something, just anything. I have no more defense than Nietzsche may have had in his time, and in saying this I plead my case in the same manner and sense he pleaded his: For instance, in *Gay Science,* Nietzsche declared that:

> One does not want only to be understood when one writes just as surely not to be understood. It is absolutely no objection to a book if anyone finds it unintelligible; perhaps that was part of its author's intention – he did not want to be understood by "anyone". When it wants to communicate itself, every nobler spirit and taste also selects its audience; in selecting them it also debars "the others". All the more subtle rules of style have their origin here; they hold at arm's length, they create distance, they forbid "admission", understanding while at the same time they alert the ears of those who are related to us through their ears p.381.

Nietzsche took this point further, which makes perfect sense to me, in *On the Genealogy of Morals* when he declared that "if this writing is unintelligible to anyone and jars on his ears the fault is, it seems to me, not necessarily mine" and stretched it in *Expeditions of an Untimely Man* when he asserted that:

> "... but who knows, after all, whether I even wish to be read today? – To create things upon which time tries its teeth in vain, in form and in substance to strive for a little immortality – I have never been modest enough to demand less of myself"

And in a timeless passage that lesser minds will injudiciously read as the ultimate testament of egomania, he thundered thus:

> I am one thing, my writings are another – here before I speak or touch on the question of their being understood or not being understood. For the time for this question has certainly not yet come. My time has not yet come; some are born posthumously – one day or other institutions will be needed in which people live and teach as I understand living and teaching; perhaps even chairs for the interpretations of Zarathustra will be established but it would be a complete contradiction of myself if I expected ears and hand for my truths already today: that I am not heard today, that no one today knows how to take from me, is not only comprehensible, it even seems to me right. Ultimately, no one can extract from things, books included, more than he already knows. What one has no access to through experience one has no ear for.
>
> Whoever believed he had understood something of me had dressed up something out of me after his own image. Whoever had understood nothing of me denied that I came into consideration at all (...)
> *Ecce Homo: Why I Write Such Excellent Books, p.1*

Indeed, it will be asking too much of me, if I am compelled to state, unequivocally and logically, what I set out to achieve or prove or declare in this work. I cannot in all honesty satisfy such a curiosity or answer such a query.

Yet, I am convinced that when I began the work, I did have certain ideas I wished to communicate, certain notions about experience, life and reality that needed deconstructing. The end product of this exercise may help in implanting in our consciousness and social practice the ingredients necessary for the liberation of thought and the un-caging of the mind in a universe already embarrassed by the over-assertion of all manners of conventionality, uniformity and orthodoxy. It may also aid the expansion of an individual's mental range and contribute in the search for a different path of experiencing in the absolute certainty that at the pristine source of the human spirit no manner of discrimination or valuation of value was contemplated, speak less of being tolerated.

I may ask, at this stage, where mankind is presently headed, not in the apprehension of the great events of our time, but in our individual and collective responses to them. For instance, it is difficult to say whether the theocratic-political resistance to cloning is weakening or not, but I do know that ultimately, nature will triumph over the snares strewn across its path.

Furthermore, classical eugenic processes may have been replaced by schools for children with special abilities and potentials, meaning therefore that, the essence of the human journey, and the measure of human progress remains the calculated grooming of human substances that will ensure the certainty of human survival in a world of so many challenges.

Equally too, I thought of expanding the section on "Chaos and Disorder", with new materials supplied by the Asian Tsunami, the Hurricane Katrina and the Pakistan earthquake, among other "Natural Disasters' that have occurred in the past ten years under the heading "Nature's Glory". In any case, I have taken the advantage of this introduction to express an inescapable truth of life: nature selects nothing, and adds nothing to itself. Its triumphal presence is but a testament of its renewal of being, its vitality and life-force.

Like all procreative processes, including birth, it comes in seasons, absorbing all the energies it can summon and master, and in so doing reveals a period of becoming that is thoroughly self effacing, unconscious, immanent and freedom-willing. The tragedy, misery and sorrow that are spawned in its wake are but a lesson that man alone is incapable of regulating the rhythm of existence; that a pristine contest between affirmation and mediation persists in our age; and that the struggle for determination yet reveals the infanthood of the human enterprise.

Over the intervening years since I began the work in 1997, the struggle for the possession of the soul of humanity has been pursued in extreme directions. The tragic events of September 9, 2001, the fall of the Taliban from power in Afghanistan, the invasion of Iraq in 2003, the rise of international fundamentalist Islamic coalitions seeking universal mastery, the emergence of a left-leaning enclave in Latin America, the North Korean nuclear imbroglio and the Arab Spring of 2011 with all the chaos, anarchy and disorder it has incarnated are indicative of the perennial conflict of values which nature spawns.

In their totality, they point to the constancy of contest between values and the various forms of mediations which this engenders: determination, over-determination, assertion, over-assertion, and disempowerment and over-disempowerment. The contradictory pulls of oppositional universal forces fairly substantiate the thesis that embedded in the core ingredients of an accentuating universal cultural monolith, are located the dislocational impulses that constantly urge for universal cultural dissonance.

Where this struggle is headed – between a fairly triumphal, constricted, universalized value system and over-assertive multiplicities of a pseudo-universal cultural base that resists this – is, of course, the subject of speculation. Our only cognitive or apprehensible roadmap in interrogating this cultural reality is to study the general and specific particulars of the production of values, all values, and to understand their specific patterns and dynamics of transformation. If this is successfully done, we will become instant witnesses not to the End of History and the cessation of all procreative social, ideological, philosophical and political processes; not even the Clash of Civilizations or the Remaking of a World Order, but inevitably the conflictual interplay of nature's elements and products, a dialectical force that exists without bounds, without limit, and that fully responds to the infinitude of experience and reality.

One other point which I will take advantage of this introductory note to stress is that, indeed, very minimal change has occurred in human experience from the cradle of human dawning to the current age that we inhabit. Nature may have become over-dressed up with an artificial garb that we call "civilization", yet the hidden impulses that direct human conduct, utterance and action have altered but little. Shorn of all the pretentiousness that collective living has engendered in a non-liberated social space, it begins to instantly appear that the artefacts of modern living – here, I am referring to the full range of technological-scientific advertisements, and the list is endless – have indeed impacted but infinitesimally on the core of human behaviour.

Take but one illustration. Have people really wondered at the conduct of two highly sophisticated corporate strategists, one male and the other female, alone in a room, who desire a sexual union and who surrender and abandon themselves to the pristine passion self-contained in their bodies, or the greed of a state functionary who must agglutinate public resources for personal use, or the hidden springs of the motivations of a global leader who directs the shedding of many lives, or even the scientific grooming and conditioning of a suicide bomber who eagerly awaits his fate?

What difference does one detect between all these and the tales of passion, greed and mass killings, in millennia past? What difference really exists between the excesses of the Roman Empire, its bestiality and hedonism, its debauchery, decadence, and barbarity and the techniques of governance in as far flung a place as Bosnia, Kosovo, Rwanda, Darfur, Somalia and such like? In the big and small things of life, in the various determinations of today's experience, across the globe, at its north and south poles, humanity excretes an endless succession of sensations, feelings and experiencing that suggest a pertinent lack of movement in mankind's historical journey.

This perception presents no social dilemma to the extent that we approach this issue from a correct standpoint: that nature can only be mastered for the purposes of man's material attainments, but cannot be subdued in consideration of all conducts that are originally human in nature. It is thus possible, intellectually, to speculate that in the process of social transformation man transforms himself; that in the process of changing his environment with the aid of science and technology man becomes a changed being. This speculative idea only rationalizes the material particulars of "civilization", already alluded to; it remains powerless in explaining the near-total harmony and logical correlation between the sophisticated bestiality of today's human conduct and the ascribed "primitive barbarity" of human behaviour in, say, six millennia past.

Because illumination, instantly apprehensible and cognitively epiphanic, is the key requirement in reading the text, I do hope that a comment or two on its structure will not harm this process or detract from the art of the pure experiencing of its content without the adding of extra, and pertinently, unnecessary value. The postscript: "Reinventing Decadence" was the first, if I remember correctly, to be written. Perceptive readers will note the polemical structure of its delivery, it's judicial, but hopefully non-prescriptivist interrogation of certain elements of universal culture and the harm an arrogant particularist mindset can pose to the autonomy of values.

Its overly harsh criticism of "America", should not be read as "all America", given the fact that within that geopolitically defined environment are to be seen forces and ideas – Noam Chomsky, Fredric Jameson and the late Edward Said, to mention but a few of such intellectuals that have been leading this charge – that present a different perspective of reality that challenge established orthodoxies. Nevertheless, this criticism stems from certain facts of cultural experience that are materially recognizable by examining the postscript very closely.

Chapters six and seven, "The Elysian Fields" and "Babi Yar" have an interesting history. They were indeed the beginning of a totally new work that I later abandoned when, just coming out of political detention in 1998, I became heavily involved with the political process that led to the dawning of civilian governance in Nigeria in 1999. That new volume was to be a companion guide to the original text on *Autonomy of Values,* its fundamental theme being the utilization of raw, materially existing historical data to exemplify the havoc done on universal cultural liberty when national political leaders cross the threshold of *affirmation and determination* of values and dwell at the infernal regions of their over-assertion and over-determination with the corresponding *over-disempowerment* of cultural freedom using unregulated *mediational* techniques.

To the extent that the logic of the two chapters fits well into the overall thematic design of the main study, I felt justified in incorporating them into its body. I am still determined to complete that companion study which, happily, I have already began working on.

The rest of the text was started and completed as one organic unit, and apart from making an additional comment on "Literary Values", I believe that they should more that speak for themselves. Literature is the greatest gift of human culture absorbing, as it does, all the elements and forces that define and determine an age. The capacity of literature to conceal certain cultural facts and over-play others means that it is neither the reflection of life not its mediation. It is life and existence as we know it, embedded in human consciousness and experience, in its capacious range, its near limitless possibilities, and its elastic and absorbent cultural and historical terms of reference. It is precisely this capacity to accommodate life, all life; experience, all experience; fact, all facts; and reality, all reality; that signifies its justification and testifies to its worth. Thus, in examining literary values, it never was my intention to examine only the values presented in literary works, but in situating such presentations to the overall cultural design relating to the production, determination, affirmation and mediation of values.

The sources of the inspiration for the work are wide and diverse; this much could be gleaned from a careful and close reading of the text. Obvious, too, is my indebtedness to, in particular, two masters of consciousness, but in an altogether unique and different context. A reading of Nietzsche's works nudged me towards the interrogation of various forms of reality, values and life-forms. He was there at the beginning of the creative process, ever-present, ever-visible to the unseen eye.

My debt to Bertrand Russell is altogether of a different nature. Apart from reading a few of his essays when I was still in high school, and knowing him to be a skeptic and an agnostic, my next decisive encounter with him was just three years ago(January, 2011) after purchasing and reading a copy of *Why I am not a Christian and other Essays on Religion and Related Subjects*.

And this was in spite of having in my possession The History of Western Philosophy and a number of other works of his without opening a single page of any of them. My joy knew no bounds in that, while my ideas, thoughts and vision of value and reality may pale into insignificance when placed alongside his eternal wisdom, I am proud to be in the company of a true master of the Autonomy of Values, a fact that made me to instantly add him to my list of "Masters of Consciousness". The piece on him and that on Luciano Pavarotti, Michael Jackson and Fela Anikulapo Kuti are the only pieces of the work written after 1998, precisely in February, 2011.

Finally, I made a promise in the introduction to *"Literature, Society and Identity"*, a work I completed about 1989, but which unfortunately is just being issued together with the present work that, increasingly, I will be adopting a multi-disciplinary frame of analysis in my subsequent works. These will be works that will help in communicating and sharing the joy of literature, philosophy, history, and cultural studies, to mention but a few disciplines, in an integrative structure of presentation. *Autonomy of Values* is the first statement in this direction. Hopefully, others are bound to follow it before very long.

Chapter 1

THE PRODUCTION AND TRANSFORMATION OF VALUES

How are values produced and transformed? Here, we must be careful to separate varied tendencies which make up an organic process. To answer this question correctly we must understand the basic differences and axiological relationships between the incarnation, transformation, affirmation, over-determination and disempowerment of values. The production of values relates primarily to the generation of cultural image-types in their pure, autonomous state. The issue here devolves around origination of values through the imprint in consciousness and material life of tendencies the requirement of whose signification is only by their existential presence. Here again, we are dealing with all manifestations of nature – its material embodiments, and those other embodiments which, in spite of their reconnective affinity with material life, establish their own presences in non-material forms.

Of interest, too, as a necessary integral component of this discourse, is the transformation of values. The affirmation, over-determination and disempowerment of values, as cultural indices, run though the whole gamut of this work and thus need no clarification here. The transformation of values, as distinct from their production, sets a term cogent to itself, not merely through declaration but essentially by the transmutation of cultural consciousness. While all values appear amoral (a positive non-value category) in their generation, transformation implies a system and structure of encoding of meaning to the extent that the presence of a value is no longer dependent on its original, autonomous declaration but as a consequence of other ascribed and ascribing cultural forces that have been worked into its awareness of being.

Re-stated somewhat differently, while the production of values pertains to their recognition as basic cultural tendencies, the transformation of values deals with the methods a state of innocence is lost as an end-product of the re-patterning of cultural evolution over a determinate or indeterminate historical time. In cognitive or perceptual term, therefore, the production of values is a declarative paradigm of culture, which implies its non-judicial interrogation in a narrative context. In the same vein, the transformation of values is an interpretative paradigm of culture, which implies its evaluative questioning in a prescriptivist context.

Individuation is a primary factor in the incarnation of values. At this basic level of manifestation, values owe no obligation to other entities in the legitimizing impulses that govern the milieu they are part of. Like other forms of life which exhibit an exaggerated individual sovereignty in their primal presences, values, all values, are not merely tolerated at the moment of their production but are appreciated as strands of existence whose autonomy or validity is self-described.

It is only through the inter-change of consciousness (derived from the struggle for material affirmation) that the meaning of values begins to transmute. The primary carrier of this transmutation process is language which, in itself, is over-conditioned by the new state of cultural independence that men have achieved for themselves.

How does this process come about? First, through the method of social engineering whereby cultural structures, including the inter-relationship between men, lose their original autonomous essence. The recognition of other cultural entities will always embody the corruption of the original state of all existing life-forms. When this occurs, there emerges a half-willing, half-reluctant subsumption of a multiplicity of contending sovereignties into a common pool of dependent and interdependent non-autonomous cultural structures. The fullest expression of this tendency is seen in well articulated human society in which an over-determined state structure enacts legal codes and statutes for the conduct of human affairs.

Another way this state of collective dependence is achieved is through mankind's later historical acceptance of its non-sovereign status on earth. Even though the belief in God, the devil, demons, spirit entities, and extra-terrestrial intelligence is an organic expression of man's capacious cultural consciousness, a stage arrives which produces not only a tenuous relationship between the material manifestations of culture with its non-material incarnations (religion, mysticism, occultism, etc.) but equally a near total separation of the elements of terrestrial nature from the infinite, eternal agencies that give the earth its coherence.

In a situation in which man is but a part of a wider creation, a very dependent part, that is, and in which that creation is, in turn, incarnated and controlled by an absolute consciousness, however understood or interpreted, with a set of immutable ethical, moral, theological and sometimes legal injunctions that are binding, the existing values must, of necessity, lose their substance, coherence and authenticity in relation to those immutable laws. The only way they will stand as recognized values and enjoy the force of affirmation and even over-determination is through a direct attunement with those immutable laws.

Man and the cultural values that are spawned on earth thus lack originality and meaning in their primary incarnation on earth for earthly incarnation of values is, in fact, a secondary incarnation, having already been produced or generated in heaven or some such place. This kind of values, and they cover virtually the whole spectrum of cultural awareness, are immediately transformed at their point of production either as affirmable or disempowering cultural elements depending on their relationship with those immutable laws. (Check, for instance, the 10 Commandments of Moses which separates cultural elements into the categories of good and evil and their later double transformation by Christ into the simple obligation of loving your neighbour as thyself and loving God, notwithstanding the particulars, motivations, lifestyle and inner feelings of your neighbour towards you; and an injunction which is a negation of the original Mosaic testament of a jealous God who will visit the abominations and iniquities of "sinners"; that is, erring members of the community, down to their fourth generation).

Cultural activity is not spared in this assault for as an element of man's non-sovereign will; the relative particulars of varied cultural expressions must be totally attuned to the absolute values that are of non-human origin or production.

In a pure cultural context, values are never anticipated before their presence is announced. It is only through performance – and the range, intensity and frequency of such performance is inconsequential – that a value becomes incarnated. Thus, values are primarily produced by individuals who exhibit attitudes consistent with their idea of survival through affirmation. When many more people exhibit the same cultural attitudes consistent with their notion of affirmation, they are seen as contributing to a pool of values whose sanction derives from their common assent. When the same body of individuals enter into a social covenant or contract and decide to abide by its regulating tenets, they not only lose their originality as primary producers or incarnators of values, but also the autonomous existence of those values which are individually produced.

This becomes the second highest demonstration of the loss of individuation, the highest being a situation when society as a whole becomes a victim of external aggression (colonialism, imperialism or defeat in war, for example) in which case the totality of its individually produced but collectively sanctioned values are thoroughly disempowered by the over-determining values incarnated by such successful aggressors.

We have already indicated the amorality of values in their original cultural presence. The reason for this is not far-fetched. The element of individuation means the ascription of self-contained valid codes within a given value to the exclusion of the relevance or validity of codes external to it. Thus, if a given value is self-contained and performs affirming functions, its value is self-stated without the recourse to other affirming values for legitimacy. In this context, therefore, the ethical or moral implication of value; which is in fact reducible to the following equations: good versus evil, right versus wrong, just versus unjust, equitable versus inequitable and relevance versus irrelevance derive from either cultural interchanges or the spiritualization of culture (transmutation of the material manifestation of culture into a distinct, separate, extra-terrestrial incarnation). It is only at these realms that values begin to imbibe ethical or moral meaning and significance, and through that the allotment of reward and punishment based on those ethical impulses.

In a more practical sense, what we have been discussing above may be stated as follows: A, B and C are three individuals who live in stone-dwellings a short distance apart from one another. For food, they gather fruits and hunt animals. For clothing, they adorn leaves and animal skins. No language is common to them, and though they occasionally meet in the pursuit of their separate goals, they hardly recognize one another's presence. However, in the course of his hunting, A's stone-fashioned weapon nearly kills B who happens to be hunting in the same forest. C almost at the same time makes away with a gathering of fruits he sees on the wayside not knowing that A placed them there.

The following day, B sees A in the forest about to hunt, goes to him cautiously and demonstrates with sign about his narrow escape from death the previous day. After a while, A understands and equally demonstrates that it is unintentional. Both nod in agreement and separate to continue their hunting. On his way home, A sees C and accosts him about the missing fruits, but tears a branch of a creeper and sticks it on top of the fruits he has gathered. Both grin and nod in agreement. From that day, A's fruits are always marked by a branch of leaves stuck atop them and are never mistakenly taken away, and no further accident occurs in the forest.

Meanwhile, in spite of the cry clap of thunder and blinding flashes of lightning, the rains refuse to come. The common stream they usually take their bath and drink from becomes broken up into ponds. Soon enough, only one large pond still has water inside it. Before long, they learn how to draw water for drinking before plunging in to take their bath for the water tastes better that way. They are now used to communicating effectively with signs and can even utter a few words and expressions they commonly understand.

When the water is nearly finished and they hardly can bathe or drink, they sit close one evening, watching the raging thunder and streaks of light produced by the lightning. Suddenly, A dashes into his stone-hut (they are sitting close by), brings out a live deer he caught that morning and, nodding to the other two, slaughters it over a heap of stones in front of his hut. He does this looking at the sky with the other two, who are busy muttering some words that then do not mean exactly anything. For three evenings, they repeat this ritual. On the fourth evening, the rains come and before long the stream begins to flow again. Every evening thereafter, they always gather at the same spot to mutter the same words, while looking at the sky.

Nevertheless, after a while, a large forest fire comes and wipes out all the animals and the fruits. The rains even refused to come down again. They gather their precious possessions and set out on a journey into the unknown. After about one week's brisk walk, they come to another stone-dwelling and see a man roasting an animal over fire. They make greeting motions that are not acknowledged.

They move on to a distance and build three stone-dwellings close to one another. Before long, they realize that their new settlement has, scattered in no particular order, over 15 stone-dwellings made up of men and women who do not communicate with one another, who injure one another accidentally, who take one another's possession and who go hungry during the season of drought because they do not know how to mutter words to the sky.

In a very short time, A, B and C stamp their authority on the settlement and though it takes them time, teach them how to demarcate their hunting grounds, identify their fruits and other possessions and offer thanks to the sky. One year later, 4 of the women deliver babies, though no marriage is contracted. In 20 years the tiny settlement of 19 dwellers has grown to over 100 people who now live together, with A leading them in their evening offerings.

They also devise a means of allocating duties: the women seem to know how to care for the children and prepare meat and fruits better; some of the men are better at hunting while yet others excel in the gathering of fruits and firewood. And because A, B and C came together, they decide that children should not be produced amongst them. The others begin to emulate this for those who develop better friendship amongst themselves declare that children should also not be produced in their midst ...

This kind of account, as highly hypothetical and simplified as it is (it does not intend to resolve the complex processes and patterns of group formation and cultural interchanges), may explain certain methods in the production and transformation of values. And as social and cultural relationships become more binding and self-reinforcing, new values which are, in turn, incarnated, bear a collective, non-individuated stamp.

Out of these newer value forms emerge the conditioning force of social obligation and responsibility as a consequence of the disempowerment of those original, autonomously existing individuated values by those other values already over-determined by collective sanction. If the new social community follows the example of the original group we hypothesized about and intensifies its appeal to the sky, the stream and the forest and derive results from so doing; and if strange cries at night lead to death in the morning or during day time, and prayers are offered to night and day in return, the group begins the process of even devaluing its collective values in favour of a new structure of values based on that dependence. It may even get to a stage in which the sky, the stream, the forest, night, day and certain animals are called by name, are revered, and have shrines built for them ...

However, value formation based on sacred writings are of a different nature altogether. Here, nature is a design, an organic entity with ascribed meaning and hierarchical functions. The engine is the Godhead who provides all answers to human needs and who has the design of existence fully developed in (his) consciousness. The earth is merely a theatre for testing out this design, like the Garden of Eden, which is complete with all the ethical logic and structure of creation.

Good is already known before creation, while bad is punished as sin. Unification with the Godhead is only possible through the affirmation of good, or through repentance, purification and atonement. Unlike values whose sovereignty is only dependent on their primal individual incarnation in a culture driven by material instincts and impulses, values incarnated by the Godhead are immutable and unchanging. They not only resist the element of individuation; they equally defy the force of transformation. Their autonomy is self-declaration. They have no need for affirmation or over-determination.

They render other values worthless and irrelevant and, in a cultural sense, stand as an absolute demonstration of the incapacitation of material life in relation to extra-terrestrial agencies. Such total disempowerment of material culture has become the greatest carrier of humanity's helplessness in the search for independent affirmation, and the purveyor, too, of mankind's present state of cultural infancy in spite of all its scientific, intellectual and technological attainments ...

However, cultural will is a stubborn entity. While transcendental cultural consciousness has spawned a world of perfect nature complete with all sanctifying immutable values, man remains at heart a product of material life. To this extent, he will keep on producing and transforming values which are consistent with his determinate material needs while at the same time insisting on his covenantal union with divine spirits.

The spiritualization of culture has led to the production of untransformed values with ultimate claims. Man accepts this, either in the context of religion and theology (atonement of sin through an intermediary for ultimate eternal harmony with the Godhead), or in the various mystical schools that emphasize the legitimacy of material reincarnation of previous lives, several realms or planes of existence, extra-sensory capacities, etc. Or this may equally be seen in other autonomously existing cultic assemblies that deploy transcendental consciousness or intelligence for the achievement of a state of spiritual harmony.

In spite of this, man still believes in the inherent capacity of the material values he produces to achieve for him a sustainable level of affirmation. And here, we are not discussing man at his primary level of cultural articulation but the so-called evolved species of mankind with their dedicated armies of devotees. We are speaking of gurus who own all sorts of "gross matter"; a euphemism for private jets, luxurious homes, yachts, state-of-the-art cars, golden robes and other material artifacts.

The Catholic, Anglican and Methodist churches remain multi-billion dollar spiritual empires with private jets, priceless art objects, palaces and well-furnished holiday resorts at the disposal of the spiritually exalted and evolved that head them. The same applies to the army of televangelists and fellowship preachers who count money in sacks, live in opulence and enjoy the good things of life. The same too applies to parapsychologists, faith healers, telekinetics and other spiritual healers the world over. They too participate in the recreation, circulation and utilization of material products.

Of course, material values are dismissed as an irritable necessity, as debasing cultural products that are needful for efficacious proselytizing. They are contemptible values that cannot be dispensed with if the far reaches of humanity must be penetrated by evolved beings who though "they are in this world, are not of it". This reasoning is plain kindergarten stuff for beneath the scaffold of spiritual illumination lurks a very imperative material quest.

Man began life as a cultural entity, and the world remains his primary realm of material incarnation consciousness. He recollects no other life outside that into which he is born. The values he produces and transforms are essentially material in nature even in their transcendence, for he always has material images in all his spiritual illuminations.

Ultimate values, incarnated by an absolute transcendental consciousness, may well remain valid as a testament of man's immortal instinct, yet they remain legitimate only to the extent that they lead to the affirmation and even over-determination of material values. Going by this, the primary source of all values is the incarnation of nature through a system of material culture. This remains the main engine of value-production and value-transformation notwithstanding the several affinities between a universe which is adjudged constricted in consciousness and its spiritual extension that answers to the call of infinitude.

How are values produced and transformed today? In precisely the same way they have been produced and transformed thousands, if not millions, of years ago from the cradle of human history. At the primary level, modern man demonstrates an acute consciousness of his cultural heritage. Whether these material artefacts are reposed in the collective unconscious in the Jungian sense, or whether they are articulated in the material contents of dreams sustained over a long historical period in the Freudian sense, or whether they are manifestations of genetic transfer of information deeply imbedded in human cells from generation to generation, contemporary values are still incarnated through the process of individuation.

This may well explain why the taking (always read as stealing) of property belonging to others always occur on a minute by minute basis (in man's original state property is a dormant, non-affirmative value which could be possessed in an indeterminate pattern or form), or why incestuous relationships (sanctified by some cultures and abhorred by others) is still a cultural reality. It may be worth noting that stealing as an aberrant social behaviour (some thieves, not all, are ashamed of their act when caught, maybe as a consequence of their subservience to the dominant operational moral ethos of their environment) is a product of cultural evolution out of which original, individuated autonomous values are disempowered by the ascendancy of social communities which establish their own collective affirming and over-determining values.

This of course does not negate the dormant validity of such repressed values provided that their affirmation is in that aid of basic material needs. However, for the Masai ethnic nationality, a man's worth is still measured by the number of cattle he "rustles" during a cattle raid, while for certain other cultures, the highest honour and respect extended to a revered guest is the presentation of one's wife to him for sexual communion.

Nevertheless, the competencies of individuated values are presently hampered by the complex networks of totalitarian social and cultural structures. Nowhere does man exist alone as a sovereign entity, and because he is over-dependent on the imperatives of over-determining and over-arching state-structures, his individually incarnated values, once they run counter to the impulses of the collectivity, are speedily crushed at the completion of the production process by an extensive apparatus of the state's coercive arms: the police, secret service agents, the judiciary and the military. Thus, it may be correct to state that though man still harbours remnants of his original procreative techniques (in the generation of values), he is presently overwhelmed by the overbearing, massive reach of the society that he is either willingly or unwillingly part of.

Yet, some values are end-products of social or cultural protest and dissent, and provided that they achieve a state of legitimacy in terms of the size of followership; and notwithstanding their recalcitrant disposition towards the *status quo,* are not merely tolerated as valid values but may also become, at a later historical date, constituent units of "orthodox" values. A ready example is lesbianism which began as a sexual protest against male sexual domination of women but is today regarded as a healthy sexual preference in the ruling circles and among the cultural elite in the Western world. Homosexuality, bisexuality and heterosexual anal intercourse are other values worth mentioning in this regard.

Nevertheless, the danger inherent in today's collective values is not just its appropriation of legitimacy and orthodoxy to themselves alone, but also that their system of production is most inequitable. I mentioned this in the section of this work dealing with "Nature and Super-nature", the bottom line of which is that:

i.) Collective values in the international system is nothing short of values incarnated by dominant members of the system, for example, the will of the USA becoming inter-changeable with the will of the UN, the international community and the whole of humanity;
ii.) Such a will serves not the purposes of all the constituent units within that system but the specific purposes of these dominant entities which, by over-affirming their values, consequently devalue and disempower the values produced by less assertive entities who are, in turn, compelled against their determinate, affirming drives, to accept such over-asserted values;
iii.) This tendency is replicated at the nation-state level where the will of incumbent authority structures is translated as the will of the whole nation and its millions of inhabitants whose own individuated wills are devalued and disempowered by such structures;
iv.) At the primary, individual level, the production of values thus becomes a hazardous exercise for what meaning does a value have, if it can neither be affirmed or even over-determined given man's inability to carry through his individuated values; and
v.) Finally, the assault against individuated values of a helpless mass in a nation-state and a helpless collective in the international system is a negation of man's cultural consciousness and survival strategy for through this is lost one of the sacred gifts of nature and culture: the autonomy of values. With this loss begins a process, as witnessed today, of man's non-cultural, non-individuated and thoroughly disempowered existence.

We observe too another cultural tendency in the incarnation and transformation of values in the modern age. Deriving from the earliest forms of divine right of kingship and the moral infallibility of the institution of the papacy, we note in our age, in their various transmutations, an incandescent form of value-production based on 'material transcendence'.

The power of life and death wielded by monarchs and despots of old are translated in the modern age into a systematized production of ultimate values by representatives of various authority structures. Even though the personalized exercise of the prerogative is sometimes de-emphasized, the final attributes of such values are not remarkably different from those of classical despotic outfits.

In very many nations today, presidents and heads of government utter words which not only carry the weight of law but even determine who lives or dies. They also exercise what is called the prerogative of mercy whereby death sentences are commutated as fancy possesses them. In other societies, there is the legislated transference of this exercise of will either to a judge or a jury that has the competence of pronouncing executable death penalty.

Like God, a judge or jury sits in judgement over other men and based on the "evidence before him/them" decide(s) who lives and who dies. Thus, the value of life and death is produced with ultimate sanction via a reward and punishment mechanism that safeguards and protects society's ruling structures. The final appeal may be to the highest court of the land or to the benevolence of either a State Governor or a President whose marital crisis or other personal problems (including being irritated by the irascible behaviour of a beloved pet in the morning) may well determine how this prerogative is exercised.

One of the highest manifestations of this transference of authority is to be seen in the Catholic Church where many ignorant parishioners believe that the priest indeed has the power to forgive "sins". Because many penitents believe that reading the appropriate Bible passages and saying the prescribed prayers will absolve them of blame, they will continue "sinning" because a producer and transformer of value – the priest, who is God on earth – will always be there to absolve him of all misdeeds.

Presidents, state governors, judges and priests are modern day producers of ultimate values; or at least, of values whose affirmations are institutionally prescribed. Yet, beneath this transcendental exercise of power and will lurks a profound crisis of culture: those who corner power – political or theological – must always erect statutes and structures for its protection, not in the furtherance of man's cultural liberty but for the repression of cultural values inconsistent with their exercise of power. To the extent that these other values, thus repressed, lose their autonomy, coherence and validity, to the extent that such a will to power becomes a monstrous drive unbecoming of the true human state ...

Chapter 2

CULTURAL REINVENTIONS: BELIEF, FAITH AND THE IMMORTAL INSTINCT

I

If belief is the articulation of consciousness in an ideal condition, then faith pertains to the affirmation of hope not of things with concrete properties but in the justification of transcendental knowledge. In the Christian religion, the idea of transubstantiation of 'sin' is the second impulse of belief; Christ's divinity being the first. In that religion too, the challenge of eschatological terror is conquered through Pentecostal revelations. While other great contemporary religions subscribe to different moral idioms, the particulars of belief and faith remain the same, unchanging and immutable.

What, however, is conveniently unassumed is that because these two ideal conditions have been appropriated almost exclusively by ecclesiastical discourses and theological ideologies, they become alienated from the depth of cultural values from where they were abstracted. To restore balance to the world of matter and value system with regard to these two tenets; which is the same as stressing the re-connective coherence of history and the cultural norms it generates, is to assert the validity of organic reinterpretation and revaluation of the material properties of existence, no matter its content.

Any belief system that is separated from its experiential sources must triumph over existentialist despair by either the means of the transmutation of thoughts into an extra-terrestrial realm, or through the self-conscious and self-contented denial of any other reality beyond the comprehension of that belief system. The first imperative is of a cosmic nature with a creative and recreative order; the second, the absolution of self from the collective determination of needs.

The ingredients of the first order are the possibility or even certainty of life after physical translation. Once that assumption is unchallenged, the idea of belief and faith as elixir remains sacrosanct, while its dislocation could lead to a whole series of moral and psychic crises in the world of believers, hence the stubborn inclination to the justification of belief and faith on parameters far removed from earthly reality.

For the second order, the denial of belief and faith which is not anchored on solid matter, and after a thorough, empirical assessment of material values leads inexorably into the acceptance of "realism without limits", to rephrase Roger Garaudy's pet expression, or to fling oneself into the haunting seduction of "morality without bounds" – a condition that only makes ethical chaos a distinct possibility, and moral anarchy a foregone probability.

Yet, history instructs us that behind all manners of belief and faith – if they must be meaningful and consistent with the idea of progress and humanization – must lie certain concrete or material indices that connect an age to another. The evolution of belief and faith in this regard must therefore subsist on the self-mutational dialectic of affirmation and de-affirmation, and assertion and de-assertion, in sequences of rapid but well-regulated succession of values that owe allegiance to their material determinations.

Belief and faith are thus constitutive parts of cultural values to the extent that they harbour basic cultural instincts which they oftentimes deny. Therefore, the proper starting point in the study of belief and faith involves different categories of restorations: the fact that belief and faith are determinants of history; the fact that they are cultural products; the fact that they must connect with material things; and the fact that they must be liberated from moral, ethical and ecclesiastical prejudices.

Belief and faith are, properly speaking, cultural quantities of hope that anticipate, reinforce and sanction the conduct of men in the process of their justification. To exist otherwise will entail a just labour of revaluation – which philosophers, literary artists and cultural theorists have been doing for centuries – for this act of reinvention stands opposed to the fossilization of thought and perceptions that have beclouded mankind's moral horizons for thousands of years. To believe in something and to have faith in the efficacy of that thing is nothing but a measure of self-awareness of the possibility of endurance and ultimate survival derivable from an idea, an icon, or a measurable reality.

Nietzsche anticipates the need for the liberation of cultural values, of which belief and faith are parts thereof, in *Beyond Good and Evil*. Yet, at this stage in his philosophical development, his insistence was on the essentiality of cultural revaluation; that is to say, a transition from a chaotic moral order to a formative amoral ethics; and a translation of universal moral anarchy into the equality of all cultural persuasions.

To Nietzsche, then, at the stage of *Beyond Good and Evil*, moral particulars are determinate cultural products; the value that is ascribed to them and which forms the basis of social regulation is nothing but deep-seated prejudices that achieve legitimacy through propaganda and collective delusion. Even in his later works, including *Thus Spoke Zarathustra,* the inescapable feeling persists that in spite of the transition from revaluation to affirmation (Superman, Will to Power, Eternal Recurrence of Events, etc); he was still seduced by the burden of moral clarifications, and not the liberation or at least the autonomy of values. But this is a whole different question altogether.

However, the question facing mankind today is not merely the study of the determination and mutation of cultural values, e.g. belief and faith – though this is vital – but the reinvention of cultural practices to achieve the needed autonomy of values. Autonomy here is not just a matter of independence via the reconnection of several traditions, each existing separately, but the liberation of the attributions of values from their delusive, narrow-minded and dangerously constricted ethical moorings. The end-product of this process will impel though and action to seek not only the ascription of new meaning and essence to old idioms, but the incarnation of a cultural platform that is pre-determined by the necessity of the needs of individuals and their various societies.

Literature, of course, provides a wide vista on which the experience of both the danger and tragedy of cultural conditioning (belief and faith), on the one hand, and the autonomy of cultural values, are tested. I will take but a few examples. When Raskolnikov in Dostoyevsky's *Crime and Punishment* decides to murder the old pawn broker, he has the belief that he is not just doing any wrong in ridding society of a miserly vermin but the faith that his act will benefit a large number of people who desperately need material help. His mental illness and moral guilt explain the collapse of his belief and the worthlessness of his faith as a result of his deep, subconscious moral conditioning.

His confession of guilt, new moral courage and self-reinvention are equally products of a new state of being that define an altogether different autonomy of perception independent of his old value projections. If he had remained resolute in his old thinking and steadfast to his old moral loyalties, after the murder, without the descent into mental agony and torture, he would still have achieved this autonomy of value irrespective of the particulars of his act. In *Crime And Punishment* then, two apparently self-contradictory moral paradigms adequately explain the essence of the liberation of value: an ethical reincarnation not dependent on the necessity of an un-actualized belief and faith, and autonomy of perception that exists beyond the morality or amorality of a pre-conceived social act.

Equally too, the destinies of Okonkwo and Obierika in Chinua Achebe's *Things Fall Apart* explain this situation well. Okonkwo's suicide is not, strictly speaking, the consequence of the collapse of his belief system and faith in the timeless efficacy of his traditional ways for he achieves a tragic kind of autonomy of value through a precipitate action that challenges the overwhelming capacity of a new socio-cultural paradigm. He dies, no longer a believer in the magic of the old ways, for its impotence has already been affirmed, but with faith in his new, re-invented self, death by suicide, which tramples underfoot one of the most potent cultural values of that old order (suicide as abomination).

For Obierika, the moral question is of a different kind. What constitutes his own liberation of value is not the obvious pragmatism of a cultural adapter, but the fact that he no longer owes any allegiance to any cultural practices – old and new – apart from the need for self-survival. His self-survival instinct, as against any noted adjustment to the new ways, constitutes his moral self-expression. He exists as Obierika and no other, with belief and faith, not to any commonly held cultural norms, but to those norms that are adequate to his autonomous or liberated moral existence.

Another good example of this autonomy of value is the character of Mugo in Ngugi wa Thiong'o's *A Grain of Wheat*. What is usually described by literary scholars as Mugo's strength of character and moral heroism (his admission of guilt with all its attendant social consequences) is in fact nothing but the distance he creates between his act and his new moral state. Mugo's new ethical awareness stems not from the possibility of exposure (this plays but a minor role in his moral transformation), but a conscious decision to achieve a new state of being which denies the perceptual legitimacy of mass feeling and collective consciousness and identity.

The problem with modern Western existentialism, particularly the variant that descends into absurdist nihilism, is its in-alertness to the specificities of autonomy of values. For when values are liberated in all human conducts, a willing meaningfulness emanates out of cultural and social practices. Such meaningfulness, in turn, negates the notions of "laden abomination", "anti-heroic sensibility of the modern age", "chaos of existence" and "existentialist angst and terror". This is so because a necessary authenticity is oftentimes conferred on any state of being, at the precise moment when it transits from instinctual impulses and responses to cognitive consciousness and affirmation.

This is the point missed in the apprehension of the human condition. In such works as Albert Camus' *The Plague* (the irresistibity of disorder and annihilation); Samuel Beckett's *Waiting for Godot* (belief and faith on an imperceptible essence); Franz Kafka's *The Metamorphosis* (a parable of the translation from man to beast); and Andre Gide's *Man's Estate* (de-affirmation of the validity of a breaking yoke whose violence will usher a new world). If the principal characters in these works were made to understand their new states of consciousness, they would have willingly induced happiness and self-fulfillment within the social conflicts, tensions and crises that pre-determine their universe.

It is perfectly possible that Sisyphus could have found joy in his unending labour if he is able to transit into a new plane of existence in which is situated the autonomy of values. His unceasing toil would have been meaningful in spite of the divine supposition of punishment. His tragedy stems, then, not from the labour he is incapable of escaping from, but from his inability to adapt a new meaning out of that enterprise. Camus did not realize this point in the *Myth of Sisyphus* – in his attempt to incarnate that fable as a justification of the existentialist despair of the modern age.

Even worthy cultural theorists of present times, including Edward Said *(Culture and Imperialism)* and Ngugi wa Thiong'o *(Moving the Centre)* still make the mistake of seeing Western imperialism and its cultural and intellectual ethos, and prescriptivist paradigms as the primary source of the contamination and stereo-typicalization of values. Even though the fact remains that America today stands accused as the peddler of decadent cultural values which have ensnared mankind in their constricted permissiveness – thus there is the urgent need to move the centres of cultural affirmations in favour of a multiplicity of cultural validities and legitimacies – the values spurned by imperialism and which overwhelm the victim remain authentic in their continual justification. New autonomous values can indeed emanate, not merely by denying the reality and inter-penetrative reaches of imperialist cultural persuasions, but by the achievement of a completely different state of cultural affirmation that resists the meaningfulness of such re-colonial cultural values.

Belief and faith must thus become re-integrated into mankind's cultural awareness of self, and draw their imperatives from the specificities of individual and collective affirmations, in order to be composed as constitutive units of new autonomous values. Their present day legitimacy must therefore be predicated, not on ecclesiastical rationalization or theological justification, but on the solid stem of new cultural ethos that does not bear the discriminatory stamp of anti-cultural ethical and moral legislations.

II

The ultimate design of any kind of existence is always the consequence of value. Here, cultural regularity performs an assigned task; that of inter-breeding of ideas and perceptions in a series of well-ordered historical successions. The highest value; that is, the most autonomous value in culture, is the law of maintenance. Its attributes are therehold: the element of preservation, which pertains to awareness of being, and the place of constant becoming in the universe; the force of perpetuation which relates to the constancy of enduring; and the factor of immortality, wherein lies the instinctual apprehension of infinite reality.

The interrelatedness of these three variables does not dissolve their hierarchical ordering in man's scale of value. Consciousness plays a decisive part in these cognitive affirmations: to exist is to preserve; to preserve is to perpetuate and to perpetuate is to attain the height of immortality. In the material sense, biology and environment are the factors of pre-determination; in metaphysics this is achieved through a conscious attunement of being to the Godhead through which a state of divinity is secured. However this issue is approached, the only objective design in life is the design of survival to the exclusion of other pre-determining social and cultural forces and impulses, which it subjects to itself and makes utterly dependent on it's hidden imperatives.

In fact, eugenics would not have become an ethical issue had Social Darwinism not become a social and political theory. Man's unregulated procreative potentials wouldn't have been questioned in spite of the quality of the species that he spawns. Yet, in spite of David Bohm's *"Human Nature As The Product Of Our Mental Model"* and Raymond Williams' *"Social Darwinism"* in *The Limits of Human Nature*, the key idea in existence is the p.p.1*[1] idea; nothing else matters whether it emanates from objective intention (consciousness and mental models) or ends at the point of affirmation (Social Darwinist action context which may in fact negate those mental models).

Today, eugenics is no longer in vogue in ethical and cultural discourses; cloning is the current RAGE. However, the amoral selectivity of eugenics – in the service of a healthy, intelligent mankind – has been supplanted, or even repressed by the immoral in-differentiation of cloning. While the former seeks for the preservation, perpetuation and immortalization of a select human species, the other in its biophilic excesses urges for an unselective replication of just any species, including inferior stocks.

Between eugenics and cloning has always been the gentle contradiction of euthanasia. If eugenics is existential infinitude via selective means; and if cloning is the immortalization of human experience via replication, then euthanasia is nothing but the regulated termination of exhausted species, human and non-human. The terminality of euthanasiac condition is a sure sign that existence can only be sustained if it constantly sheds its burdensome load: preferential suicide, mercy killing, etc. could provide the necessary elixir for the continuance of existential journeys. These are however issues that would be revisited.

Previously, philosophers have tended to mutate the ultimate autonomous value in life – the p.p.1 idea – into tiny, contradistinctional particles, through a mediational process that lacks actual social or cultural basis. The way this issue is handled in literary practice will be examined subsequently.

Though Friedrich Nietzsche created a new thesis of value – the *Will to Power* – whose reconstructive originality eventually gave way to other social renditions (the will to happiness, the will to pleasure, the will to success, the will to perfection through self-assertion, and ultimately the derived image and identity of the Superman), the debate had gone on for thousands of years before him. For Socrates and Plato, the ultimate value of existence is the search for a conducive ethical order wherein justice, truth, good governance, and hierarchy (recall Plato's assertion: I am happy I am born a man not a woman; a free born not a slave; a Greek not a Barbarian; etc, and most importantly the differentiation of authority in *The Republic* which only a philosopher king will lead) will reign.

For Aristotle, the value of existence is an unclassified will to power (primitive in relation to Nietzsche's latter clarification, because man is inherently a political animal). While Immanuel Kant believes in a moral world order in so far as he stresses that things may exist in themselves but will only inherit value in the process of collective determination and mediation of causes; Arthur Schopenhauer avers that the reality of existence is the constant negation of the tragic state – a cultural value – which itself unwillingly succumbs to the idea of tragedy.

Yet, beneath all this philosophic constructions lies the inescapable social and cultural fact of all times: the will to preserve, perpetuate and immortalize. A moral world order remains ordered only in the constancy of its affirmation; that is, self-regulated continuance of idea made fact. Things will only retain their collective quality in the process of renewal; that is, self-perpetuation by other means. Man remains a political animal if he still has a family, community or state to grasp and hold; his very political quests, contests and endurance are the instinctual facts of his desire for immortality. There is nothing more succinct that explains this instinctual search for immortality than the will to power. However, what is willed to become, as a consequence of overcoming (strivings, testing, questing, self-mastery, etc) is not power in itself, but power to effectuate existential victory. It is not fame or wealth, but the capacity to triumph over existential odds.

Philosophic mutations and mediations of value that suit a time-bound cultural requirement are inadequate to grasp and explain the meaning and essence of the p.p.1 idea as the ultimate autonomous value in life. What they succeed in doing is to produce a near anarchic typology of value systems in their isolation, solitariness, and in the absence of their re-connective idioms.

What explains man's place on earth is not his desire even to eat, urinate, make love, acquire power, etc, but his need to perpetuate his state. If these tendencies and habits help to realize that desire, he places a value on them (for example, a Zen-Buddhist monk who lives an ascetic life may never place value on food as a factor of perpetuation just as a Hare Krishna devotee will regard meat as a path to unhealthy life and spiritual death. But this is not so with regard to the over-stressed military dictator in an African state, or a well-fed, robust-looking president of a Western country).

As an autonomous value, the will to perpetuation harbours no ethical or moral illusion; this has no meaning to it in terms of the strategies of existential survival. What is imperative; that is, the only correct and factual instinct is the desire to preserve. Once attained, every other thing must become part of its affirmation. It is to this extent that it becomes clear that the only worthy design of life on earth is the paradigm of self-perpetuation and self-succession; the moral dilemma attendant on it (for example, killings, wars, murders, etc) is only incidental in its scope of meaning and significance. Even for the priest, the theologian and the rulers of secular states, this moral question is in itself a strategy of survival, a mechanics of self-perpetuation of their varied stocks at the expense of the rest of humanity. This however is another issue altogether.

Now, we go back to Biology, bio-ethics, and man's perpetuation via procreation. Only few people move society – others just exist. If we re-examine the issue of the reproduction of species, especially with regard to self-perpetuation (of which eugenics and cloning are part), we will not be startling mankind with an original cultural insight; we will be merely asserting a fact of existence long denied. Anti-cloning legislation is a reaction against man's desire for immortality, and because it runs counter to human nature, is bound to be ineffectual.

Many people fail to observe this with regard to political philosophies. The political ideologies that eventually became extinct derive their loss of legitimacy out of the rebelliousness of man's inner instincts which will forever oppose all manners of legislations and moral injunctions. Fukuyama attempted to explain this with regard to the collapse of orthodox, bureacratized communist structures in Europe, (that is a non-legislative Marxist dialectics in opposition to a legislative Marxist political doctrine), but falls into the same trap in pinning all his hopes in a legislated liberal democratic order.

It is thus obvious that cloning and eugenics will remain attractive, though currently marginal, options open to a self-perpetuating humanity in spite of the anti-cultural assertions of theologians, members of the priestly class and pretentious leaders of governments. The only reasonable concern that ought to be demonstrated pertains to the realm of indifferentiation of this self-perpetuation assertion which is the same as asserting the invalidity of an unregulated immortal instinct.

The fact remains that the future of mankind can only be guaranteed not by the reproduction of just any form of human species (presently this involves the biological responsibility of over 98% of the human stock), but through the careful selection of a qualitatively higher form of species that can utter new words in the next millennium. This should be the organic essence of procreation, self-perpetuation and man's immortal instinct.

What may not be directly obvious to many people is that literature provides adequate insight into man's immortal instinct; that is, his desire for self perpetuation. It is a characteristic which defines all literary ages. Oedipus killed the old man at the place where three roads met because he felt his sense of survival threatened. He saw the riddle of the Sphinx as an affirmation of the Theban people's desire for collective preservation. His relentless search for the murderer in their midst is projected as a patriotic service in honour of social, spiritual and cultural continuity unaffected by pestilence and divine wrath.

Antigone, too, dies because she sought to immortalize her brother in a non-biological manner, which only an honourable burial, in opposition to Creon's anti-self-perpetuational legislation, will guarantee. Creon, on his own part, by denying another person's right to immortality, is motivated, in the main, by his desire for preservation and self-continuity.

We see this with regard to Agamemnon apparently sacrificing Iphigenia on the altar of collective security and preservation of his armada, and Orestes avenging his father's murder as a pre-condition for his non-biological immortality. Patroculus died on the plains of Troy as a consequence of his reckless search for self-perpetuation which a victory over Hector and the other Trojan princes would have conferred on him. For Achilles, the picture is totally different, because he consciously insisted on a limited life-range on earth in favour of everlasting name (an immortality he eventually achieved even down to our own generation). In all these references, myth plays very minor role, being, as all literature is, the reproduction of mediated reality that lies deep in man's objectively determined imagination and consciousness.

Macbeth may have been motivated by considerations of political power in his murder of Duncan to usurp the Scottish throne. Beyond that however, all his other subsequent acts are occasioned by a self-perpetuation instinct, which to him has become an autonomous value. It is interesting to note that, to the very end, with imminent death staring him in the face, as it were, he is still propelled by the idea of indestructibility and immortality, as delusive as that notion may appear to the rest of us who suspect or know otherwise. What is true with regard to Macbeth equally holds in the case of Dr Faustus, going by Marlowe's and Goethe's accounts of his earthly quest and divine intuition. The list is endless, down to Raskolnikov in *Crime and Punishment,* Buzanov in *Fathers and Sons,* Gregory Melekhov in *Quiet Flows the Don,* Doctor Zhivago in *Doctor Zhivago,* and the chief characters in *Nineteen-Eighty-Four, The Plague* and *Lord of the Flies.*

Closer home to my native Africa, the literary craft of the continent's principal literary artists is replete with this notion of self-perpetuation and instinctual immortality – as an autonomous value. In Chinua Achebe's *Arrow of God*, it is clear that Ezeulu's appropriation of instinctual divinity – a kind of Oedipal quest – is a necessary part of his desire for transfiguration into an immortal essence. The subsequent psychic and spiritual disasters that this causes is meaningless in consideration of the necessity of that human desire. The same is true of Sam in *Anthills of the Savannah* whose ascription of a benign Godhead leads to a whole series of social disorders and political instability.

We see this also in the image of Bakayoko in Sembane Ousmane's *God's Bit of Wood;* in the character of Ben in Meja Mwangi's *Going Down River Road;* and in the spiritual epigones in Ayi Kwei Armah's *The Healers*. In fact, Ngugi Wa Thiong'o's over five decades of literary labour is dedicated not merely to the historical documentation of Kenyan people's individual and collective heroism, but their desire for immortality, personified in such characters as Dedan Kimathi. That self-perpetuating image dominates his works (Waiyaki in *The River Between;* Boro in *Weep Not Child*; Kihika in *A Grain of Wheat;* Dedan Kimathi (as his historical self) in *The Trial of Dedan Kimathi;* Karega in *Petals of Blood;* Muturi, for example, in *Devil on the Cross;* and Matigari in *Matigari*).

It is clear that the immortal instinct, which includes any preservative and perpetuational assertion, is an autonomous value in man's estimation of self. As a principal law of nature and cultural survival (the biological necessity is already taken for granted), its attunement to human nature must be continually emphasized. The battle for man's dominance on the planet earth, against all other challenges, cannot be won by narrow-minded, self-limiting bio-ethical legislations which hamper the exercise of this will. What ought to be championed is the cause of biological regulation of succeeding and even supplanting species, in order that the cultural affinity between a primeval instinct for immortality and the present day self-perpetuation consciousness is constantly affirmed.

It was a near misfortune watching Dr Lan Wilmut, the biologist who led the research team that cloned Dolly, the sheep and Rev. Jerry Fawler, the Founder and Chancellor of Liberty University on CNN's Larry King Live on Wednesday 25 June, 1997 discuss cloning, bio-ethics, biotechnology, genetic engineering and the moral and legal implications of replicating exact species. It was a near misfortune because I saw an apologetic (repentant) Dr Wilmut virtually declaiming the significance of such a tremendous breakthrough in biotechnological research.

I felt sorry that he didn't quite appreciate the range and fundamental thrust of his scientific endeavour. He was at pain in agreeing with Rev. Fawler that cloning should not be extended to the human stock; that the idea was not an attempt to create a race of supermen and women; and that the then President Clinton's declarations on the subject was not a subversion of nature.

The fact remains that human potentials are near inexhaustible in terms of breaking down the boundaries of unconquered nature. The direction of this assault may be the subject of ethics and morality – as narrowly constituted and understood as they presently are – yet the debate over nature, man, culture and the environment has little to do with the subjective susceptibilities of individuals no matter their temporary power and influence. The urgings of consciousness which find affirmation in social practice demands the most resolute exercise of liberty and freedom of will in all cultural interchanges. Cloning is not and should not be the subject of discussion in comic shows (which Larry King Live oftentimes is) for the simple reason that it emanates out of existing nature as a coherent and not a deviant statement of its inner law.

If any discussion indeed should become part of its constitutive scientific agenda it can only be tolerated in the areas of emphasis, perspective and the overall necessity of harnessing its organic end-results for the improvement of the human stock, human happiness, cultural practices and man's perpetual dominance in and of the universe.

In the raging debate over the bio-ethical implications of cloning, I am quite convinced that nature will ultimately assert itself over the over-determining impulses of the present anti-cultural ruling political and theological-religious castes in the world. I am also convinced that the cultural factor of affirmation of basic values which imposes no handicap on the relative autonomy of all life-forms will, in the long run, define man's preservative quests and his instinctual search for immortality. Part of this logic of nature is not far in coming.

Not too long after Dr Wilmut's declamations, I read in a Nigerian daily, *The Guardian,* an account of an American scientist's desire to begin the process of human cloning. That account which derives from agency reports, detailed the scientist's declarations as follows:

> An American physicist, Richard Seed, has set a target to produce 200,000 human clones yearly as soon as he gets the process right. Each clone is to initially cost $1 million but it is expected to cost less afterwards.
> Addressing a formal press conference after he shocked the world last week by declaring his intention to clone a human, Seed, a 69-year old scientist, said: "when I was seven years old, I was brilliant and crazy. I don't mind being called crazy".
> The scientist explained that the initial market for human clones would come from the 10 to 15 percent of infertile couples who cannot conceive by alternative means such as test tube fertilization or the use of surrogate mothers.
> He said that between 5,000 to 10,000 couples in the U.S. would initially benefit from the project. Adding: "it's my opinion that after that, it will be

200,000 couples a year".

Very little profit, he said, is expected on the first successful clone, because it will cost about $1 million to produce. He, however, added that the cost will reduce dramatically and profits would be made thereafter.

"Profit is a desirable word, profit is essential", he said, adding: "Every human activity has to make a profit".

If the U.S. bans human cloning, he said, "we're in the process of arranging an off-shore location" to proceed. He said that his choice would be Tijuana, Mexico while one of his colleagues prefers the Cayman Islands, another, the Bahamas. He disclosed that he already had a medical team lined up but did not name the members. He was however reported to be broke and is trying to raise between one million and two million dollars for the project.

While scientists in Scotland used a mammary gland cell to clone Dolly, the sheep, he said he would use a white cell for a human, employing an electric current to initiate cell division. For the patient, he said, it would take about 40 seconds to implant the embryo, with no anesthetic, adding that "science has much more experience with the human embryo than other animals", making the chances for success high.

The Guardian Monday, January 12, 1998, pp. 1-2

This fairly long account of Richard Seed's testimony is necessary because of the deep-lying cultural issues it invokes. For a start, while man's immortal instinct is actualized through the replication of the human species, such a process, programme or project should not be in the aid of "cultural humanitarianism" (helping infertile couples whose expressed genetic characteristics will be of tremendous benefit to humanity, and not just their families or immediate communities.

Again, the "shock" that greeted Seed's declarations is

understandable given the over-determining will of a tiny but powerful ruling political and theological-religious caste which have distorted and illogically transfigured human cultural values and human civilization after its narrow notions of ethics and a moral world order.

Yet, another contradiction in Seed's testimony is his manifest dependence on existing cultural mores for the legitimation of his scientific innovation. He wants his project to be a profit-incarnating one, thereby appealing to the greed and avarice of corporate strategists who are prepared to cast off their "moral handicap" (they will repent of their sins thereafter in the numerous churches and fellowship gatherings that abound nowadays) and invest their capital in it once all the practical, economic cost – benefit analysis has been undertaken. Seed is thus not a true promoter of the real cause of humanity – careful selection and replication of superior human species that will mould the engine of new history and culture in the millennia to come – but a scientific trader who wants to graft on a purely scientific material the determinants of his material culture. If anything, the cloning project should be the affair of governments or a well-funded, non-profit – making consortium empowered by governments with the express responsibility of searching out the carriers of eugenic consciousness and intelligence for universally beneficial selective replication.

Without realizing it, Charles Krauthammer, in a *Time Magazine* essay, "Of Headless Mice... and Men", enters the record books as a master of illumination by bringing to public attention the potentially limitless possibility of bio-technology in fulfilling man's quest for immortality. His understanding that science has the capability of creating "unconscious" life to aid the full and efficient functioning of "productive" life is one of the most potent cultural statements of our age.

If we disregard his anti-cultural illusions regarding man's preservative instincts; his excess of hysteria; and his near

56 ■ AUTONOMY OF VALUES

absolute dependence on a constricting universal ethical order erected by a jealous ruling caste, as organs of thought, what remains of his insights is a studied concession to the original design of man's existence – an innate quest for immortality founded on a deep-rooted cultural instinct.

Let us sample some of his thoughts:

i. "When prominent scientists are prepared to acquiesce in – or indeed encourage the deliberate creation of deformed and dying quasi-human life, you know we are facing a bio-ethical abyss. Human beings are ends, not means. There is no grosser corruption of bio-technology than creating a human mutant and dis-emboweling it at our pleasure for spare parts".

Response:
A human mutant is an inarticulate, un-affirmable entity. Its consciousness of self is non-existent. Such a bio-technological creation can thus only assist in realizing the potentials of beings that are already incarnated with full awareness of self, and particularly that group of mankind whose exercise of will is not directed at self-affirmation but at the resolution of challenges that face the future existence of mankind.

Let us take an example. If three scientists who are on the verge of discovering a vaccine against the AIDS virus are to be involved in a road accident, and the condition of whose continued existence is dependent on multiple organs transfer that only bio-technologically created human mutants could readily provide, what will constitute the core moral and cultural question in relation to the future happiness of humanity?

The obvious fact – not the truth – of the matter is that Krauthammer's standpoint is a sum product of the ethical prejudices of his cultural milieu, particularly the reverential treatment of the human body which is directly patterned after the image of "God", to the extent that a loss of one of God's own creation imposes a damaging ethical burden on the millions of beneficiaries whose collective empowerment is dependent on that loss. Krauthammer's standpoint is thus neither scientific nor cultural in its material sense, but rather a romantic allegiance to culture-in-transcendence – which in its own expansive though problematic context is a form of legitimating man's immortal instinct.

ii. "The prospect of headless human clones should put the whole debate about "normal" cloning in a new light. Normal cloning is less a treatment for infertility than a treatment for vanity. It is a way to produce an exact genetic replica of yourself that will walk the earth years after you're gone".

Response:
I do not know precisely when and why man's quest for self-succession has become an idle, vain pastime. Man has always demanded of himself the cultural competence to outlive his determinate realm. Religion speaks volumes about this. In material life, his exploration of this principle has created for human civilization immortal icons from where references are always drawn. The author of the works of Shakespeare is surely not materially aware of his immortality, yet, he remains an immortal icon. So are Plato, Aristotle, Marx, Nietzsche and Freud.

Now, for man, the possibility is opening up for the translation of his capacity for immortality from a future prospect (at which stage he is materially unconscious of that fact) to a material condition in which he can affirm that possibility in his lifetime, and he is called vain. Here, as before, the scientific-cultural issue in cloning is not and should not be tailored to suit the productive and replicative nuances of just any human stock or gene pool, but must be directed at the careful selection, replication or sustenance (via bio-technological mutation of "still" life) of advanced human species. Here, again, as before, infertility or humanitarian gestures should play no part nor achieve any relevance in this cultural process.

iii. "The headless clone solves the facsimile problem. It is a gateway to the ultimate vanity: immortality. If you create a real clone, you cannot transfer your consciousness into it to truly live on. But if you create a headless clone of just your body, you have created a ready source of replacement parts to keep you – your consciousness – going indefinitely".

Response:
Man created the original immortal instinct by transferring his consciousness of transcendence from an unrealizable material realm to an extra-terrestrial plane of divinity. Since that creation, his consciousness has been focused in one direction – a self-preservative quest that has taken him to religion, mysticism, occultism, and, today, in the new age occult groups. This has been his pristine cultural wish – to live forever, in eternity, and to sustain his awareness of self in life-after.

Now, at last, he has within his grasp, a certain reversal of his immortal instinct: he can actually re-translate his wish from a transcendental plane to a material one. Cloning is the first step; the second is the replication of unconscious life from where conscious existence could be extended indefinitely. Man is thus on the verge of a major scientific-cultural breakthrough which will make nonsense of his puny efforts in dieting, healthy living, physical fitness and obsession with vitamins and anti-ageing mendicants. And someone calls this ultimate vanity.

Who in fact among us will really desire death (a source of immortality-in-transcendence) if indeed he could live in eternity on earth in full health, and in full possession of his consciousness and other capabilities? If this point must be re-stressed, we will come to the inevitable conclusion that the passion for immortality will be fed with more than a dose of narcissism. It needs a stronger narcotic – the narcotic of cultural preservation, and with that the endurance of individual and collective human species. And because this passion is in favour of natural laws and logic, it must always keep aflame man's consciousness in whatever direction that it finds space, in spite of all legislations to the contrary.

iv. "Congress should ban human cloning now totally. And regarding one particular form, it should be draconian: the deliberate creation of headless humans must be made a crime, indeed a capital crime. If we flinch in the face of this high-tech barbarity, we will deserve to live in the hell it heralds"* (all quotations from *Time Magazine,* January 19, 1998 p.56).

Response:
I wonder who "we" are really! Surely it does not include scientific researchers, bio-technological experts, medical personnel, beneficiaries of the cloning process, etc, all who must be living in the twilight zone of the prevailing moral orthodoxy, all who must be indeed mad, and all whose sense and idea of culture and self-preservation must be indeed weird and out of this world. Krauthammer addresses no real scientific or cultural issue here. His sense of loss is nothing but the pathetic outpouring of a man unaware of the real essence of values, all values, particularly the value that nature has jealously incarnated in its own primary image; the value of man as a cultural product, and the value of culture as man's permanent, irreversible search for self-preservation, and ultimately, for immortality.

However, while the debate over the bio-ethical implications of cloning, as a consequence of mankind's present state of cultural infancy (read: a repressive and illusory "moral" world order) will not end today, what must be re-stated is that man's immortal instinct will never be served by the indeterminate, unselective and random replication of 5,000,

10,000 or 20,000 ordinary human stock, but by a rigorous and painstaking cloning, and the replacement of vital parts from life-mutants, of a determinate number of men and women drawn from superior gene pools.

Chapter 3

FIVE LIFE-FORMS

i. Nature and Super-Nature

The notion of "alternative living" is repugnant to nature. CNN producers and presenters missed this point when they began airing on Monday, 20 October, 1997 a week-long programme on "alternative living", which was ostensibly meant to address varied ways of life, practices and value-systems that supposedly fall outside "established orthodoxy".

The point that is missed, and precisely the tragedy of the Western intellectual, philosophical and scientific thought over the centuries, and which is parroted by scholars in nation-states that fail to exercise the autonomy of intellectual value, is that the idea of "alternative living" is the repression of apprehended reality for all living is an alternate of another and, in an undiluted, autonomous sense, orthodox to another. The dilution, repression and partial selection of life-forms may not only be an indication of cultural arrogance; they point at a deeper crisis of value: the inhibition of value via a historical process is passed on as the evolution of universally sanctioned standards of living, when in fact what is foregrounded is a narrow-minded illusion that wears the cloak of conventionality.

All value-systems; that is to say, all forms of living are equal to another, occupying the same scale of orthodoxy in an autonomous context. To speak of "alternative living", for example, alternative medicine, is to assume that a particular system of medical practice has been conferred an indisputable legitimacy to the extent that other medical forms which fall outside its terms of reference must then occupy a curious, exotic, peripheral and, oftentimes, inferior spectrum in the evaluation of medical practice.

However, the fact of life as against the truth of a value system holds that the legitimacy of any life-form is measured by its determinate efficacy, not for all people, but only in affirmation of the goals set by members of its "constituency", so to say. To this end, the credibility of life-forms does not depend on the "adding of value"; which is to say, that their authenticity is not, after all, dependent on the determination of their inherent value in relation to their responses to life situations.

For when a value is added to certain life-forms and denied others, hence emerges the absurd categorization of tradition, mainstream, convention, "natural things" and orthodoxy on the one hand, and "alternative living" and super-nature on the other. A way of life is the recognition of impulses and instincts which must be actuated; once a measure of satisfaction is derived from such a way, its value becomes autonomous and self-established and is recognized as such. Its existence as a way of life or as a life-form no longer depends on its acceptance by those outside its range of legitimacy; in the same way that it must tolerate, in equal measure, as legitimate, the expression of reality in that other way or form. This equality of life-forms, thus, dispenses with the separation of life-matters into dominant and marginal typologies, and secures for all forms of existence a necessary authenticity that is inherently conferred on all autonomous values.

What I have been discussing with regard to "alternative living" is in essence a translation into a related quality of the brilliant argument in "Romeo's Error: a Matter of Life and Death and Nature and Super-Nature," from where I took my title. For if mankind were to accept the existence of "alternative living" as opposed to either orthodox, conventional or traditional life-forms or practices, it must also be seduced into accepting the separation of reality into nature and super-nature. Nature, in a non-liberated, non-autonomous sense will then pertain to the regulation of values universally communicated and commonly shared by the human race, while super-nature or preter-nature devolves around the incarnation of images, idea, or impulses that lie outside such a regulation of value, or to be more precise, outside "legitimate reality".

Therein dwells the "shock" of drama, as an extraordinary event, whose connection, as an individualized attribution of meaning to the universalized particulars of existence, is nothing short of being tenuous. The trembling balance between drama as a hidden and overt intimation of conventionalized super-nature – the expression of which is the restoration of individual action to the sanctioned legitimacy of universal conduct – is reducible to the calculation of reality in terms of what is or that appears natural in relation to what is or that appears unnatural or supernatural.

However, no matter how hard an investigation occurs in this field – and scientists, social and natural, are obsessed by it – the fact of life again proves once more the dissolution of reality into a large, loosely coordinated mass of autonomous natural values. The supernatural import of reality is a determination of will and consciousness and not an empirically derived modal testament; that is, if empiricism is short of its restrictive intellectual usage. To escape the snare of ignorance – the means whereby what is or appears natural derives its vital energy, force and authenticity – an absolute value is cast on limited will as the ultimate exercise of all will. When this is done, all other forms of life whose persuasions and significations are not accommodated by the above attribution are mercilessly rendered worthless – that is to say, not cognizable, inscrutable, and abnormal.

To act is to express a certain form of will; and to act is dependent on the degree of consciousness and strength. Para-psychology, psycho kinesis, transcendental knowledge, extra-sensory perception, etc mean nothing in themselves, and should mean nothing either to their promoters or detractors, for the specific reason that no nature is transcendental and no energy or perception extra-sensory, provided that a connection exists between the expressions of these autonomous values and the material world they inhere in.

For to admit their extraordinary essence is to separate nature against itself; it is to accommodate the vulgarization of reality which Western "natural" science has been doing for nearly 3,000 years now. It is to legitimize the imprisonment of values by specific histories and cultures, and to declare with little wisdom but excessive noise, that there indeed exists a dissonance between the varied manifestations of autonomously existing forms of life in nature and the inherent, authentic values they purvey.

ii. *The Naked State (Liberty and the Natural State)*

The distance between glamour and the naked state has little to do with elevated living and the condition of innocence. The first only expresses a cultural and moral disease, while the other inhabits, within its undiluted essence, the spirit of humanity. To be naked is to be pure – and here purity pertains to a value which is already in itself autonomous and free-floating. To be glamorous is to dress up corruption in the garb of sophistication for no difference exists between the moral excesses of a highly prized sex worker and the assumed depravity of a street hag.

Here, however, I speak of corruption not in the sense of an unethical value, but rather as an expression of moral hypocrisy. The village maiden, unschooled in the art of masking her inner essence, should or ought to command the same attention as a super model or the film star in the eyes and consciousness of those who reduce femininity to unsubtle sensuality. It is thus the addition of "unnecessary value" to the condition of being in the former – exclusive residences, high-flying, "cosmetics" (meaning exactly what it is), and interaction with "polite society" (euphemism for tolerated debauchery) – that imposes an unwarranted aura of artificiality which separates such an entity from the pure humane value of a rustic milk maid. The same is true of the village chicken thief who steals as a survival strategy (in Ngugi's position in *Devil On The Cross*) he is even a better species of humanity than the elegant robber who will trap air in bottles and sell to the masses or the corporate hound who steals in front of a PC in several stock markets.

The value ascribed to glamour, and this attains an unreal height in the prize the glamorous commands – high fees in modelling, film and TV roles, corporate deals, etc – is not necessarily a value that means anything, for man's true spirit may lie in a good bath – in the absolute condition of nakedness – and at which point must dissolve those inhibited, unautonomous values that separate people from themselves.

Man's naked state is not a parable of his historical, biological and cultural inheritance, for if the clothes he wears serve only a functional purpose, for example, as a protective coating against the vagaries of the elements, then his state of nakedness may be seen as the truest measure of his inner worth or value. To judge a man or a woman on the strength of his glamour and outside the intimations of his or her real essence, is to deny the value of existence which only the naked state can declare. And for a better clarification, the cultural milieu which harbours such pretensions of glamour and seeks to pass them off as the accumulation of needful values is in itself in want of self-examination, and in the process of self-destruction by posing an unnecessary challenge against the original meaning of existence.

Take a uniform, for example. A uniform should serve as the classification of value, and not its justification. For when the cloak of a priest or the tunic of a soldier, to cite but two instances, is ascribed a value beyond the immediate legitimacy of such a profession or vocation, the end result is the constriction of other values not accommodated by such cultural expressions; that is, the emergence of a system of thought and belief which places a higher value on certain "attitudes" of life. The challenge this poses to cultural freedom, and the resistance it engenders, can only be counter-smarted by the consistent affirmation of the equality of all values variously reflected in the diversity of clothing forms and modes. In this regard, such a resistance may not even work, for the ultimate resolution of the crisis of identity may be the restoration of man to his original state of being – wherein true equality could be and is readily achieved.

The justification of value may also produce an extreme reaction in the imagination of cultural thinkers, as in the case of *Leo Tolstoy* who, after observing the bestiality, empty pomposity and arrogant swagger of soldiers in his day (and in our time too) opines that "military service always corrupts a man, placing him in conditions of complete idleness, that is, absence of all intelligent and useful work, and liberating him from the common obligations of humanity, for which it substitutes conventional considerations like the honour of the regiment, the uniform and the flag, and, on the one hand, investing him with unlimited power over other men, and, on the other, demanding slavish subjection to superior officers". (*Resurrection*, p.76).

Tolstoy's argument, which I readily share, is that the overvaluation of the profession of soldiery which manifests in the ascribed importance of its uniform is in itself its inherent worthlessness as a value, for to relate to others on the basis of superiority as a consequence of the uniform, any kind of uniform one wears, is to scream aloud the insecurity of one's own value, and through that, to announce the dehumanizing potentials of one's vocation.

Tolstoy also handles the true naked state in his apprehension of the incorruptibility of "atmosphere" as a reflector of unshared experiences. Though I have my problem with his insight which I intend to demonstrate, he did successfully underscore the essential ingredient of the equality, and by extension, the autonomy of value. Tolstoy's position is that:

1. The value we ascribe to our conduct is pre-determined by the atmosphere we inherit and dominate;
2. That value-judgements is determined by this partially selective inheritance;
3. That those we condemn for engaging in valueless conducts, in turn condemn us because they too have inherited and dominated other atmospheres not within our shared experiences; and
4. That the equality of value should stem from an objective assessment of all life's atmospheres and situations independent of the subjective intimations of our consciousness.

This is the way Tolstoy presented his case:

> Nobody can wholeheartedly do anything unless he believes that his activity is important and good. Therefore, whatever a man's position may be, he is bound to take that view of human life in general that will make his own activity seem important and good. People usually imagine that a thief, a murderer, a spy, a prostitute, knowing their occupation to be evil, must be ashamed of it. But the very opposite is true. Men, who have been placed by fate and their own sins or mistakes in a certain position, however irregular that position may be, adopt a view of life as a whole which makes their position appear to them good and respectable. In order to back up their view of life they instinctively mix only with those who accept their ideas of life and of their place in it. This surprises us when it is a case of thieves

> bragging of their skills, prostitutes flaunting their depravity or murderers boasting of their cruelty. But it surprises us only because their numbers are limited and – this is the point – we live in a different atmosphere. But can we not observe the same phenomenon when the rich boast of their wealth, i.e. of robbery; when commanders of armies pride themselves on their victories, i.e. on murder; and when those in high places vaunt their power – their brute force? We do not see their ideas of life and of good and evil are corrupt and inspired by a necessity to justify their position, only because the circle of people with such corrupt ideas is a larger one and we belong to it ourselves.
> (*Resurrection*, pp. 201-202)

The only problem I have with this demonstration of life's more than one atmosphere is that in the true naked state, wherein values are free and autonomous, such statements as "knowing their occupation to be evil, must be ashamed of it", "placed by fate and their own sins or mistakes", and "because their number is limited" are unnecessary. They betray an attitudinal disposition that is consistent with the justification of certain values over others. Beyond the elemental force of chaos – in value – system and cultural affirmations – which I suspect lies beneath Tolstoy's inhibitions, must endure the quality of equality of values for the legitimacy of the quoted contentions in a genuinely liberated state of existence if essentially questionable.

In determining the limits of values which Tolstoy sees as the interdependence of opposite qualities: good and evil, kindness and wickedness, energetic and apathetic (*Resurrection*, pp. 252-253) harboured by a human entity, care must be exercised in locating defensive consciousness as the end-result of cultural tyranny. For while it is true that human beings exhibit contradictory properties in relation to experiencing, these properties are non-classifiable with regard to their value: they exist as autonomous properties with immanent originality. Their commitment as life-forms is to the value of experiencing and not to the exigencies of their consequence.

This issue is worth reflecting on in the naked state, for men and women have always allowed themselves to be pushed to the margins of existence, whereby they begin to not only question their philosophies of life, but to negate them, tortured, as they are, by self-doubt, guilty feeling and harassment of conscience by a cultural establishment which seeks to monopolize orthodox, conventional and legitimate conducts.

We see this in the Stavrogin-led nihilistic group in Dostoyevsky's *The Devils,* who surrendered the legitimacy of their programme of spreading chaos and disorder as a basis of building a new Russian society to the ideas of the complacent enforcers of the social, cultural and political status quo, and in the Bazarov-led anarchist group in *Fathers and Sons* who are manipulated into a virtual renunciation of their ideas by a generation that has severed any meaningful dialogue with them.

In these two situations – thousands of others abound in literature, history and philosophy – the emphasis ought always to be on the protection of value systems outside their authentic spheres; and the resistance to a cultural monolith that attempts to subsume a pure, naked state into its narrow stream of though and action. Yet, this is a matter that cannot end at this point.

Note on the Pure State

I don't particularly care for thriller or adventure films, but watching *Dante's Peak* was a real excursion into the meaning of the pure state and the true essence of value. Beyond the substance of titillation, the real dimension of the film is the expression of the purity of nature and natural phenomena – here expressed in the form of an earthquake and volcanic eruption. The sheer impact of quake or an eruption is the ultimate expression of its life-force. Such ecological conditions are not an inherent negation of men and beasts being, at the level of consciousness and articulation, unaware of their existence.

When they express the autonomous values they harbour, they do so in utter disregard of its consequences on other values and life-forms that are impacted upon and subsequently, disempowered. To this extent, therefore, they constitute not the elemental objects of annihilation as many will have us believe, but a necessary renewal of their life essence in the specific condition in which they acknowledge only their own presence.

Man's capacity to arrest the potency of such forces for his continued relevance in the universe is only salutary to the degree that the value which he carries must also be continually reinforced and perpetuated in the conflict between autonomous realities. Man must thus struggle against these forces not because they are evil or destructive or an indication of divine wrath or ecclesiastical rapture, but plainly because to fail to do so will be a concession to the invalidity of his own universal presence against the challenge of other pure value-carrying presences. This point, I think, may also be important in the consideration of the naked state.

iii. *Sex and Existential Rhythm*

One of the greatest moral burdens of the current age is the place of sex and sexual conduct as an expression of value, and yet this need not be so. As a life-form, sex stands in equal relationship to other autonomous values; that is to say, the legitimacy of sex as an incarnation of meaning is established beyond the dictations of conventional ethical wisdom which imposes authenticity on it only on the basis of the assertion of love. The crippling effect of this form of dictation is seen in the inherent substitution or even transmutation of two distinct values: the value of love and the value of sex, which of course must exist as free choices in the scale of social intercourse.

While love is not essentially the vulgarization of sex via social and cultural legislation mindlessly accepted by the bulk of humanity, it is surely a form of over-determination wherein its assertion on the one hand is the disempowerment of another value category on the other. To avoid this moral crisis is to constantly affirm the distinct, separate, free and pure existence of these two life-forms, and to acknowledge their independent capacities as the expression of values devoid of moral or ethical implications.

However, I hasten to add that the shedding of the burdensome moral cloud under which sex is presently wrapped in order to see it as a form of life whose relationship with other life-forms is only at the level of the interdependence of autonomous values, has nothing to do with the sexual permissiveness of Western societies. The latter case is a social and cultural situation which I have already classified as the inessential or rather tragic expansion of the boundaries of permissible, legitimate social conducts on which such social and moral conducts such as sodomy anchor their authenticity and significance.

The fact of the matter, if it must be re-stressed again, is that in spite of all genetic postulations – and Western scientists are daily examining genetic materials to make their case worthwhile – these sexual forms, usually classified as alternative sexual orientations or preferences, are nothing but a protest against the constitutive nature of society. And as protest, they become forms of over-determination of value; that is, the new sexual value they exhibit no longer has a place in consideration of the original autonomous value of sex.

They are surely an indication of the transition of one value (sex) into another (protest), occupying as they do an inter-determinate experiential boundary as a consequence of that very over-assertiveness. In more plain language, the reason why Western sexual permissiveness is not a pure life-form is that while there is a liberation of the sexual act and conduct, such a freedom is usually not in the service of sex in as much as the original decisive propulsive force is non-sexual in nature, being a conflict-based mediation of the specific political, economic, and a whole lot of other complex social structures and character of the state.

If man's experience of history is anything to go by, it becomes readily manifest that humanity's sexual consciousness has been dealt severe blows by two distinct, though interlocking forces: religion and cultural conventions. The first of this has considerably succeeded in not only mystifying its original natural essence, in favour of a restrictive moral sanction (sex as pleasure, as play, is sin; it's essential purpose is procreation), but also by the process of transmutation of values whereby sex is made to lose its autonomous existence, it has instilled in man the obligatory rites of self-abnegation. Flowing from this, sex is portrayed as a value which in itself is valueless; its legitimacy can only emanate through a conditioning process of denial and negation, except on the basis of non-biological, ethically sanctioned necessity.

Culture takes off from where religion lets off. Varied cultural persuasions acclaim the non-originality of sex as an experiential performance in a way that is not ascribed to the eyes, the mouth, the nose or the hands, and this is in spite of the instructions of psychology and psychoanalysis (here, an investigation of Freud and Jung may be a requirement). Yet, all these human components are necessary instruments which carry their respective experiential values; they stand in the same scale of affirmation in spite of all the cultural attempts to either over-determine or disempower one or the other.

Cultural norms over-reach themselves with the institution of marriage, particularly monogamy, which is nothing but the legislation of sexual behaviour. Apart from the fact that monogamy and indeed all marriages lack the capacity to live up to their self-imposed sexual "discretion", implying the exposition of the artificiality of marriage as an expression of sexual bondage, it is pertinently anti-nature to expect a man or a woman to drink water or wine from a single cup, in only one form and at only one given time, no matter his or her environmental circumstances. If water or wine must be drunk at home, in the office, in an aircraft, in a business conference, at anywhere, and oftentimes, in just any way, then it follows that sex is a need that must be satisfied in any place, at any time, and if conditions warrant such, in just any way.

As we will still discover with regard to work, sex becomes an unmanageable burden, and loses its status as a life-form when it is subjected to all forms and manners of over-affirming mechanics; it loses its creativity, vitality and instinctually derived joyfulness. Like work too, its total essence is the attainment of pleasure and harmony with oneself, others and nature, and the exercise of self-willed freedom of choice in all its particulars. To fail to do so; that is, to fail to grasp this basic freedom of conduct is not only to trap oneself in a stifling, mechanical repetitive act sanctioned by a hollow ethical world order, most often derived from a prejudicial cultural and religious structure of meaning, but to deny its very legitimacy as an autonomous life-form.

One may ask what place sexually transmitted diseases occupy in the exercise of sex as a life-form with autonomous properties. The response to this is a very simple one. Sexually transmitted diseases exist as either free or dependent entities in search of the actualization of their value potentials. That man happens to be the victim of this kind of affirmation, and that he has thus far not been able to counter this determination successfully have little to do with the issue at hand. It simply shows that as a value-carrying agent, man has been less than successful in mastering nature and the environment with regard to this specific issue.

Mastery here, it must be understood, does not relate to his over-determining propensity, but simply a natural response to the contrary affirmation of these other entities. Of course, virtually all health issues that relate to sex would have by now become obsolete if man has totally and comprehensively achieved this state of medical perfection. Thus, the issue of abstinence, monogamous sexual relationship or artificial sexual conduct (the use of condom, contraceptive pills, diaphragm, etc) have to do with this failure of science and nothing whatsoever with issues of ethics, morality or religious and cultural conventions. If one should be afflicted with a life-threatening sexual disease, say AIDS, and even dies from it, the material content of that situation does not pertain to his exercise of sexual ability and conduct without restraint, but because of the failure of science to affirm this vital life-form through sexual conduct, restraint, abstinence or monogamous sexual relationship are decisions determined by the state of science in today's world. To this extent, such decisions need be encouraged, even though such encouragement negates the law of nature, and the existence of sex as an autonomous life-force with its independent and legitimate autonomous value.

iv. Work Ethic
I have but a brief remark to make with regard to work as a life-form. However, I consider such an insight adequate enough in explaining this category of reality on which the greatest percentage of adult humanity predicates their affirming capacity. Work is commonly held to be the externalization of an inner productive possibility. Here, the consideration is not culturally restrictive or ethically bound; which is to say that the freedom work achieves for itself from the determination of morality is only expressible in the practical content of its material or utilitarian value. Restated differently, the exercise of any productive endeavour (productive meaning materially rewarding, and nothing more) is only actuated on the derivation of utilitarian end on which survival is dependent.

Yet, this insight remains a cultural illusion because work

as a form of life is a value whose autonomy is self-declaratory; its legitimacy does not emerge out of the transition from value to value; that is, from work to a material, utilitarian end. Work is therefore only pleasurable to the extent that its joy and reward are not dependent on the expectation of material reward; the only criterion of value-determination remains the act of productivity which in itself must be separated from other material determinations or injunctions.

To work is thus to express a value which carries with itself all the instincts, nuances and capacities of all values. To work is, again, the exercise of free will that is ungoverned by pressure, conventions, cultural mores, institutionalized procedures, element of comportment, obedience to authority and such other conventions and traditions which over the years have not only emasculated this elemental freedom but have thus far devalued work as a sovereign value.

The most obscene form of slavery is the predication of work on utilitarian survival or the receipt of material reward. It is slavery to the extent that its primary principle is not the loyalty to an autonomous value which work is, but to a totally different value which is utilitarian or material in content. It is obscene in that when people are compelled to work, even when they hate, despise or look with contempt at the work they do, but must however work to survive, their humanity is lost, and with that their individual and collective identity as integral units in a freedom-willing universe.

The highest expression of this universal cultural disease is in academic settings whereby contemporary universities have succeeded in producing and retaining only an infinitesimal percentage of intellectuals who nurse this hope and the bulk (over 98%) of academics who must grind their hours away in faculty offices, administration boards and lecture theatres because they must survive. This perspective should even hold for the roadside vulcanizer, car repair man, or vegetable hawker who ascribe no value to their work except on the coldly inhuman calculation that what they do derive its value only on the material expectation appertaining to it, and thus becoming a means whereby they can occasionally "polish their humanity, honour and image" by wearing their Sunday best procured from the "dividend" generated by their "work".

The highest expression of work as an autonomous value is demonstrable in various life tendencies, one of which is genuine intellectual labour (what I write now is only productive in the context of self-fulfillment; its ultimate material import is of no consequence) whereby ideas, illuminations and visions are incarnated solely for their sake, and probably for the benefit of humanity if not today, but surely in the service of a much more liberated future time, and two, in the purest expression of "genuine" pornography whereby the players derive maximum benefit from their act and regard its utilitarian properties as a secondary affirmation.

In effect, such a pornographic material must, unlike our consideration of Western sexual permissiveness, declare its stand in favour of relative autonomy and self-assertion, and if it so does, operates even beyond the capacity of intellectual self-declaration in that it achieves the unity of two autonomous and legitimate values all at once: the joy of the sexual act itself, and the satisfaction that its self-imbedded utilitarian possibility guarantees.

To restore man to his original cultural state (not an original religious state which is a by-product of a deeper, and longer historical consciousness) is to separate the value of work from the potential of utilitarian reward; that is, to continually assert the authenticity of free affirmation over either over-determination or disempowerment of values, and through that to achieve a cultural balance in the way man perceives his environment without hampering or incapacitating entities whose sovereignty are culturally sacrosanct. The failure in the achievement of this goal means, at least for now, man's in-alertness to this obvious manifestation to his cultural bondage and ethical enslavement; an achievement that may thus be set, not as the goal of the present generation, but as the self-motivating impulses and instincts of a happier future human race.

v. *Chaos and Disorder*

Chaos and disorder are two interrelated life-forms. The debates over them have been as intense and problematic as the subjects themselves; the philosophical and moral issues involved no less contentious and haunting as the incompleteness of mankind itself. Beneath all this attention lurks, probably, the greatest crisis of culture as ever can be. To escape the charge of subjectivism in their typology as autonomous values is to free oneself from the impediments and handicaps of a limited cognitive or perceptual approach. This is to assert that any consideration of the place of chaos and disorder in the human society must be anchored on the historical evolution of man. It is to dispense with the layers of latter-day moral, religious, cultural and philosophical crusts that have impeded the understanding of their inherent orientation as legitimate values; and to dispense too, with the contemporary assumptions regarding their place in shaping the future of mankind.

The present cultural situation in the world today is nothing but a reflection of the enforced conformity to all forms of asserted wills created, not only by the unipolarization of the universe (a bipolar monolith inspires no confidence in this regard), but also by the relentless zeal with which an overly conformist imagination has successfully over-determined its impulses at the expense of values that ought to exist in an autonomous state.

This has led to the emergence of cultural and social concepts that are short of their innate relativity through a process of ultimatum of values – in essence the most dangerous form of over-affirmation. Variously expressed as the will of the "international community" or as the demonstration of the imperatives of a "New World Order", the pursuit of conformity has necessarily engendered a capricious distortion of chaos and the proper meaning of disorder.

At national levels, chaos and disorder suffer even a double tragedy: the legitimacy of authority structures that perform ends suitable to this "international will", however the circumstance of their emergence, and an obsession with order, stability, peace and harmony – ruthlessly pursued – which serves not the purposes of society's affirming entities but the over-determining impulses of its leadership. This could be seen in the repression of opposition groups in various nation-states and the emasculation of autonomously existing entities that are classified as marginal and fringe cultural, cultic and social groups by a malignant orthodoxy in the Western hemisphere, particularly the United States of America.

The culture of contentment is the edification of the status quo and serves as the poisonous darts directed against all mangers of self-affirming, non-conformist impulses which seek to restrict and limit the authenticity of contentment to its legitimate zones. To this extent, the freest expression of cultural freedom, while not necessarily meaning a throwback to man's original state of individual exercise of will at the expense of other wills not recognized by specific individuals (commonly called the state of nature), will necessarily involve a considerable capacity to declare a standpoint in life and existence in so far as that declaration is situated on the recognition of the existence of other entities, the logical necessity of continuous struggle between independent values, and the balance that must be achieved between affirmation and over-determination in order to avoid the disempowerment of values.

While it is true that values, which having asserted themselves, may indeed be transformed into over-determined will at the expense of re-asserted values (e.g. again, the will of the international community which classifies nations either as rogue or terroristic on the basis of the subjective determination, and over-asserted authority structures at the nation-state level which classify the opposition as malfunctioning social miscreants, trouble-makers, enemies of the state etc.), the legitimacy of this perception lies not in its moral strength or validity but specifically on the acclamation of its triumphal presence.

Thus, if this balance is not achieved; that is, if the triumphal presence of over-determined values continues to wreak havoc on disempowered values, such values are still legitimate in themselves, and morally credible in their strategic bid to announce their own presence through struggle. Therefore, the contest between stability and chaos or order and disorder does not involve any moral category or content nor does it produce an ethical or spiritual crisis. It is rather the struggle between value-creating and value-carrying entities in search of recognition in a universe driven by an excess of over-determination and the excess of disempowerment.

Thus, the goals set by anarchism, nihilism and other philosophies and beliefs that emphasize the need of flux over cultural stability and social harmony are legitimate goals provided that their target is directed, one, against other super-imposing values, and, two, towards the attainment of specific, determinate ends. Such an end may be the free reign of all manner of cultural passions whereby society is engulfed in a perpetual search for justification, or it may be in the service of a new state of order and contentment which their over-determining triumphal presence will herald.

The success or otherwise of such an enterprise may mean either one, some or all the following theses:

i. The innate strategic incapacity of such a programme and its promoters to affirm, and then over-determine its presence;
ii. The legitimate exercise of will by the targeted values and their promoters who set about annihilating such a challenge; and
iii. Loss of belief and faith in such a programme by its

promoters who thereby confess its illegitimacy to the authenticity of other opposing values.

However such an end may be, such values are still absolved from any moral or ethical burden; the burden they bear is the burden of failure, incompetence and incapacity whose expression is their near-total disempowerment. I will illustrate these three theses from two texts: Dostoyevsky's *The Devils* and Ivan Turgenev's *Fathers and Sons*.

i. From *The Devils:*
"Asked why so many murders, scandals and villainies had been perpetrated, he replied with feverish haste that it was all done for the systematic destruction of society and the principles on which it was based, with the object of throwing everybody into a state of hopeless despair and of bringing about a state of general confusion: so that when society–sick, depressed, cynical, and godless, though with an intense yearning for some guiding idea and for self-preservation–had been brought to a point of collapse, they would suddenly seize power, raising the banner of revolt and supported by a whole network of groups of five, which were in the mean time recruiting new members and discovering the best methods of attacking the weak spots". Lyamshim (one of Peter Verkhovensky's subordinates) to police officers on their philosophy, tactics and strategies, *The Devils*, pp.661-662.

iia. From *Fathers and Sons:*
'He is a nihilist', repeated Arkady. 'A nihilist', said Nikolai Petrovich. 'That comes from Latin, Nihil – nothing, I imagine; the term must signify a man who ... who recognizes nothing?
'Say – who respects nothing', put in Pavel Petrovich. And set to work with the butter again.
'Who looks at everything critically', observed Arkady.
'Isn't that exactly the same thing'? asked Pavel Petrovich.

'No, it's not the same thing. A nihilist is a person who does not take any principle for granted, however much that principle may be revered'.
Arkady, to his uncle Nikolai Petrovich: *Fathers and Sons*, p.94.

iib. 'Then we realized that just to keep on and on talking about our social diseases were a waste of time, and, merely led to a trivial doctrinaire attitude. We saw that our clever men, our so-called progressives and reformers never accomplished anything, that we were concerning ourselves with a lot of nonsense, discussing art, unconscious creative work, parliamentarianism, the bar, and the devil knows what, while all the time the real question was getting daily bread – to eat, when the most vulgar superstitions are stifling us, when our industrial enterprises come to grief solely for want of honest men at the top, when even the emancipation of the serfs – the emancipation the government is making such a fuss about – is not likely to be to our advantage, since those peasants of ours are only too glad to rob even themselves to drink themselves silly at the gin-shop'. Bazarov to Pavel Petrovich, *Fathers and Sons*, pp. 125-126.

While the nihilists in *The Devils* are incapacitated by a combination of the three theses as any study of the text will reveal, the nihilists in *Fathers and Sons* are only hampered by the first and second theses. In fact, the nuances of unbelief; that is, the opposition to the validity of conventional principles which nudged the consciousness of the dissenting voices in the 19th century, became, in the 20th century, a cumulative cultural and moral obsession. From Andre Gide to Samuel Beckett; from Albert Camus to Gene Genet; and from Andre Malraux to the latter-day theorists and practitioners of cultural and moral individuation, the challenge of the age has been the search of distance which separates mass assumptions from the prerogatives of an individual's loyalty to himself only, if and when he is even allowed to do so by environmental and biological necessities. These forces are, in turn, held to cloak humanity with the scaffold of uncertainty, meaninglessness, anti-heroic sensibility and angst.

To this extent, Charles Mason, David Koresh and the Unabomber, to specify but three individuals and the tendencies they represent, appear as natural successors to the idea of shock as a cultural expression in Walter Benjamin's sense of the term, and this also more than validates Georg Lukacs' assertion in *The Meaning of Contemporary Realism* that modernism as a philosophical and ideo-aesthetic system is more of a contentual, perceptual and cognitive apprehension of the universe than a formalist category unrooted in the material content of an age of change. This again appears as a further legitimation of Yevgeny Zamyatin's thesis in *"Revolution and Entropy,"* Ortega Y Gasset's intellectual instinct in *"The Dehumanization of Art",* and Roger Garaudy's assertion about the limitless capacity of realism, the substance of which is the infinite apprehensibility of the resources of the artistic image which could be made to serve any end.

In a more political sense, we also find evidence of this in John Lukacs' demonstration in *The End of the 20th Century* and *The End of The Modern Age* that the excesses of Hitlerism is, in fact, organically inter-related to the evolutionary logic of Western history as nationalism and not liberal democracy or communism defined the structure, content, character and essence of the modern age in a manner previously unrecognized and unappreciated. And this is, in spite of those cultural and social excesses, including chaos and disorder, which it procreates.

Chaos and disorder are thus not a manifestation of a cultural or moral disease; neither is anarchy. As cultural properties with inherent value-capacity, they remain systems of engagement with and confrontation against other cultural expressions. The end result of such a process which, in reality, has nothing to do with the health, vitality or the future destiny of mankind, achieves significance only on the basis of their relative affirmation, excessive over-determination or relative disempowerment.

Chapter 4

ULTIMATE VALUES

Now, one way of establishing the meaningfulness of a cultural element is by identifying its inherent dependence on and inter-independence with material life. However the pursuit of meaning is undertaken, the essence of culture is the signification of tendencies which have bearing on natural laws, expansively apprehended, and freed from the stifling limitations of Western intellectual and scientific thought. We have already indicated this with regard to belief and faith, alternative living and the other various life-forms that operate as cultural products.

In a cognitive sense, this perceptual paradigm does not recognize the separation of nature or culture against itself; which is to stress that all attributes of nature, including out-of-body experiences, soul-travel, transcendental intelligence, parapsychology and psycho-kinesis, to name but a few of the so-called mystic and extra-terrestrial consciousness, appear as properties of nature with inherent value capacity.

Cultures incarnate values, and in their freest state, values exhibit only the most basic form of affirmation or determination. This reasoning which applies to most categories of value is anchored on the parameter that cultural freedom, which is realized in the purity of values, achieves significance only on the basis of the autonomy of those pure values. This system of knowledge explains, in the main, and in a basic sense, the inherent original dynamics of all cultural and historical evolutionary processes, whether in the sense of myth, ritual or man's earliest survival instincts, and his half-conscious and half-unconscious encounter with the larger realm of nature.

However, in the process of incarnation, culture-dependent values tend to establish themselves on the basis of struggle and conflict. Anthropocentrically, this could be seen in the divine struggle between the members of the original Greek Pantheon whereby the triumvirate of Zeus, Poseidon and Hades, aided by Hera supplanted Cronos and his wife, or it may be in the brutal colonization of Palestine by the descendants of Abraham acting on God's command, or even in the simple act of cannibalism whereby men overpower one another, and make food out of their flesh in justification of the instinct of survival. It may even be seen in the various animal, fairy and folk tales, replicated in an evolutionary–diffussionist manner, in various national cultures.

It thus becomes established as a material fact that the struggle between values is the mechanism, or more properly put, the organism through which their pure state is lost. The loss of purity of values is the attenuation of their absolute autonomy. It is from this struggle, carried and out in countless ways, in a thousand forms and involving millions of culture-carrying values, that emerges the concepts of affirmation, determination and over-determination, disempowerment, and even over-disempowerment.

When values achieve relative success, any value for that matter, it begins the process of affirming its existence; it is no longer pure, in that its 'being' is impacted upon, corrupted and modified in the process of that struggle, and in its new state of assertion. When affirmation is virtually completed, such a value becomes immediately over-determined, acquiring as it does so, and depending on its cultural reach, the elements of validity, authenticity and legitimacy, previously held by all values – in their original, pure state.

A reverse process is noticeable with regard to those values which, having been incarnated fail in the struggle for affirmation with other values. Therein begins their process of under-determination, disempowerment, and sometimes over-disempowerment. When this process is completed, and depending again on the cultural reach of such disempowerment, such values are not only contaminated and distorted but become invalid, inauthentic and illegitimate. Therefore, most, if not all questions of validity or its lack, authenticity or its lack and legitimacy or its lack are culture-dependent in the sense of either the affirmation or reassertion of values.

All values are thus equal in the consideration of their original, pure, autonomous state of incarnation; they only begin to lose meaning and significance in the context of a struggle which leads to either their being affirmed or disempowered. And even in this, but not in all cases, this cultural situation is mastered by the law of relativity for oftentimes a contrary reversal process occurs in which their arrested capacities may harbour the potential for the re-assertion of their buried legitimacy, notwithstanding the length of their cultural invalidity.

Here, however, we are concerned with yet another category of values which resist both the pulls, pressures and tensions of cultural change. In the theory of meaning on which the philosophical thesis of epistemology builds its planks; and in the behaviour of these cultural elements, wherein is derived the basic tenets of empirical-positivistic and phenomenological views of existence and reality, these values defy all known cultural laws of mutation through conflict. They are values whose incarnation is forever constant; whose purity is infinitely permanent; and whose autonomy and validity is such that, to borrow from Nietzsche once more, "time but tries its teeth in vain".

These values are ultimate in the sense that they need no affirmation to establish their existence; neither do they require any determining process to effectuate their triumphal presence. They are ultimate too, in that they bestride nature's two fundamental thresholds or realms of; the realm of nature's material manifestation and its transcendental orientation. By so doing, they cross a number of cultural boundaries and distances, accumulating as they do so, instincts that are social, spiritual-theological, ethical, moral, mystic and cultic in characteristics.

Ultimate values are values whose cultural reach is boundless and, in existing beyond the range of history and space, they impact upon consciousness and human perception with such a competent capability that is sustained from generation to generation and from millennium to millennium. In actuality, the highest expression of mankind's cultural dilemma, and even crisis, is to be seen in the organic behaviour of all ultimate values.

The precise reason for this is that in denying the validity of affirmation through assertion, they all become, in one form or another, over-determined in the absolute sense of the term. By disempowering other values in a self-effacing manner (they do not need conflict or struggle to achieve this end), they become cultural terrorists in that all aspects of culture, and the products they incarnate, including man who is the highest expression of this incarnation, are answerable to them in an inexorable, fatalistic manner.

The unity of inexorability and fatalism thus becomes the most profound demonstration of cultural incapacity, for when the autonomy of values is lost in the condition in which that loss is accepted as being legitimate, the various strands of cultural affirmations are totally shifted in favour of the loss – incarnating values. Therein begins the process of cultural slavery, a process which at the material plane implies the cessation of struggle against the slavery-carrying agent, and at the transcendental plane, the acceptance of certain forms of absolute cultural reality.

One of the most primary of all ultimate values is death, which in a medical sense may be defined as the cessation of all vital functions. But following on the heels of new scientific evidence, errors in clinical interpretations of death and the new functions of parapsychology, death may in fact be defined as the cessation of most vital functions in the context in which certain metabolic processes continue to operate, and the organism is capable of being restored to his/its original state under certain conditions. This definition of death and its expansive scientific thesis is to be seen in *Romeo's Error: A Matter of Life and Death,* a work I have already alluded to.

However this cultural situation is looked at, the fact of nature – at its primary, elemental and material level, is that all organisms must at one time or another cease to enhance their material capability and performance; that is, death, like when a man or woman dies, and is buried either in a dug grave or have his/her body burnt over a funeral pyre. To all intents and purposes, such an individual has thus far ceased to enhance his performing capacity on earth, and this absolute disenhancement is the ingredient on which death builds its ultimate cultural castle.

Death need not announce its presence in a visible, predictable form (it does so sometimes like when a fatal shot is fired, a rocket is launched or a dagger is stabbed, etc). Yet, however it appears, it arrests all life processes in a self-effacing, non-declaratory manner; its consequence is enough announcement of its triumphal presence. And this notwithstanding the whole layers of affirmations and determinations it disempowers; like the death of a family breadwinner whose absence may change the family's social status, material survival, moral strength (his daughters could be forced into prostitution); or in the death of a head of state which may lead to power struggle that may alter the fortunes or destiny of such a state (civil strife and war are not ruled out in this). All these forms of affirmations are thus brought to an end by a cultural agent which doesn't even recognize their presence, legitimacy or authentic existence.

Death remains an absolute cultural value in spite of all externalizing complications worked into its form and content. Such externalizations attempt to shift the emphasis from the scope of pure cultural expression into culturally indeterminate realms that are severed from their material rooting. The distance that is achieved through this process is passed on as a non-cultural one with its own autonomous orientation.

One example of this process of externalization is the idea of life after death whereby immortality or even divinity is achieved through the covenantal unity between man and God. Such an achievement is thus established as the infinitude of life and existence which limits and then subsequently overpowers the terminality of death. Death is then seen not as a cultural phenomenon but as a religious value – the punishment for man's original sin, and the hope that man will live forever after the process of atonement, absolution and the acceptance of the rites of trans-substantiation.

However, what is at play here (other plays include the recognition of existential ladders or planes, material reincarnation of old material entities, earthly divinity whose bond with immortality need not be presaged by material transition from one value-life to another value-life after death, etc) is man's expression of a deep cultural wish; the element of preservation and perpetuation through which he hopes to achieve immortality. It's an issue already investigated in this discourse.

Apprehended in the manner developed above, death is made to lose its worth as an ultimate value to the extent that it, too, as a value needs to assert, affirm and determine its presence, and in the stated circumstances is made illegitimate via immortality. Nevertheless, such cultural speculations only satisfy man's yearning for immortality, a cultural instinct that has already been overdeveloped over the intervening millennia, and a value which in itself is adjudged absolute and ultimate on the cognitive or perceptual apprehension of death as a relative value with relative affirming or determining competence or capacity.

In essence, the debate over death will continue so long as man remains a being who is obsessed with immortality, and such a debate is only healthy and helpful if it does not push cultural discourses away from their legitimate terrain; that is, that at the primary material level, death incarnates itself as an ultimate value, and that those other externalizations of this dynamics are manifestations of consciousness and assumptions that are culture-dependent.

Beyond this, any other measure of consideration of death as a non-cultural entity, is not even a question of one's subscription to the idea of belief and faith, which in themselves are determinants of culture, but the deepest demonstration of man's non-instinctual speculation about the necessity of his existence, the meaning of that existence and its ultimate justification in a manner that cannot be possibly explained by any known cultural theory. By being basically indeterminate, it calls into question man's cognitive capacity, a perceptual handicap that may still have to be tolerated given the cultural infanthood of a very large portion of humanity.

God – and the range of cultural discourse on the subject is stupefying – is of course the greatest of all ultimate values. In terms of the production and transformation of values, the idea of God, and with that, the concepts of transcendence, divinity and immortality, defy virtually all known cognitive criteria. That the notion of God is a cultural issue and that God itself is a cultural essence is beyond doubt. What however, is obscure, is the process of cultural universalization whereupon this cultural category shows a remarkable symmetry in diverse cultural milieux. This is precisely so because no lacuna exists in mankind's consciousness of the substance of the subject; a substance that is at once culturally apprehensible and cognitively incomprehensible.

No matter the analytic weapon at one's disposal, and its range is wide and profound (empirical, materialist-positivist, phenomenological, experientialist, ecclesiastical-theological, mystic-cultic, etc), the various interpretations of God are inadequate in situating such a cultural image in a wholly coherent manner. While an expansive cognition of God may compose within its limitless terms all the de-personalized forces of nature regulated by binding laws (accident, even if it is allowed, is seen as an intensive cultural element). An exclusivist-particularist approach which is most often theological in orientation specifies such an ascribed transcendental intelligence (now separated from the material content of nature) solely within the framework of a personalized being with an inflexible omnipotent, omniscient and omnipresent capacity. The nexus between these two cultural distances remains the unconditioned legitimacy of that cultural image whose notion of order is superimposed upon all reality. God thus remains the procreative agent that inspires a universal moral standard, conditioned not by the conscious will of freedom-seeking humanity but by the narrow design of established moral-ethical, theological-religious and mystic-cultic schools and systems.

Nevertheless, in the cultural value of God as a sovereign entity do we witness the greatest resistance to the understanding of how values are produced, their process of transformation, their original, pure, autonomous state, and their conflictual relationship which leads either to affirmation and over-determination (assertion of legitimacy and authenticity through triumphal presence) or disempowerment (illegitimate and inauthentic state of being through attenuated presence).

The nature of this resistance is total in that the idea of God is culturally attached to the state of universal order and stability; in that the collapse of one (God's essence as an ultimate arbiter of conduct) will mean the attenuation of universal moral or ethical standard as presently constituted. Humanism, particularly its atheistic brand, achieves no recognition as a value in this context for the promoters of this idea insist that the distance between cultural anarchy and ethical chaos can only be bridged by the triumphal presence of God as an ultimate value.

No debate over God as a value-carrying agent can ever resolve mankind's present-day cultural dilemma, and in asserting this, I call into mind three propositions:

"For God so loved the world that he gave his only begotten son that whosoever believes in him shall not perish but shall have everlasting life." Here, an adumbration of Christian theological reasoning wherein is derived: "I am the way, the truth and the light: No one enters into the father but by Me". (Ultimate, exclusivist declaration which forecloses the legitimacy of other contending theological persuasions).

The Epicurean thesis that it is either that God wants to stop evil but cannot; can stop evil but does not want to; or He cannot stop evil and does not want to; and lastly, He can and wants to; in which case if He wants to stop evil but cannot, He is not omnipotent; if He can but does not want to, He is not benevolent; if He neither wants to and cannot He is neither omnipotent nor benevolent; and if He can and wants to, how does evil exist?

Finally, we refer to Benedict Spinoza's thesis of natural and moral relativity in a de-personalized, law-governed natural process of procreation, replication and continuity of values, wherein is located the idea of the authenticity of all theological-moral systems. For example, in a very succinct response to an erstwhile student who became converted to Christianity and who flung savage words to his old master on how he has denied the Saints and will thus rot in hell fire, and how he, a miserable worm, ever believes or imagines that his religious or moral system is the best there ever is considering the other religious and moral systems that existed and still exist in different parts of the world. Spinoza thanked his former student for having found new masters and a new faith but asked him why he believes or imagines that, of all the other religions which existed and are existing in different parts of the world that his is the best.

These debates are an integral part of mankind's search for cultural meaning, and for the generative processes whereby values are produced, transformed and mediated. The real challenge for man today remains the fact that while these processes establish the criteria for the evaluation and justification of all kinds of values, any attack on the foundation of God as an ultimate value is not only considered an apostolic misdemeanour but more significantly as an assault on human civilization itself. Such incubus of passion is not only reinforced by the structure of culture and the values it carries in today's world but is self-perpetuated by the universal unwillingness to come to terms with God as a cultural force.

Until such a reflexive will is accentuated in favour of the extenuating ingredients of a stifling cultural consciousness which fails to recognize that the primacy of nature in the life of man is only expressible in not just the revaluation of all values but in their justification and liberation as autonomous entities with determinate and indeterminate affirming, over-determining and disempowering capacities, so long will cultural slavery be the scourge of the present generation ... However, such terror that man feels in his desire to free himself from a preservative cultural bondage may, again, serve the need of universal cultural infancy, leaving for the visible future the competence to chart its own course towards cultural liberty.

Apart from death and God, man, as a cultural category is also an ultimate value, or at least seeks the ascription of such a value. How he does this – apart from his very deliberate quest to master nature by breaking through its layers and frontiers, and thereby systematizing his consciousness and knowledge of its composite entities to his own advantage (civilization, and all manners of progress in medicine, science, technology and communication) – is through the already investigated process of immortalization through preservation and perpetuation. The affirmation of the various wills that pertain to this has already been demonstrated, chief among which is eugenics and cloning.

However, man is incapacitated by a number of cultural impediments. Death remains a cultural challenge, not a biological necessity, and it has not been successfully challenged. Man is also caught squarely in the paradox of his own self-preservative cultural creation: while he searches for immortality, he remains unable, or even unwilling to deploy the cultural weapons at his disposal for its achievement. He is weighed down by his own self-created cultural values which he does not want to revaluate and liberate, because such a revaluation will lead to the collapse of his cherished cultural and ethical illusions about a universal moral world order.

Such an illusion is seen in the haste with which he condemns euthanasia as selective genocide via elimination of unpreservable and unproductive human stock and cloning as an unselective and undifferentiated replication of human species with all the assumed bio-ethical issues that are involved. Yet man will remain a cultural pretender in his search for immortality unless and until he utilizes the two weapons at his command – the selective germination of superior species (eugenics), pursued alongside their careful replication (cloning). And until he does so, the idea of man as an ultimate value remains a mere idea, not only in cultural discourses but also in the realm of nature.

Finally, inconsistencies in nature emanate from the force of interdependence. Etiological relationships in themselves are end-products of these inconsistencies. The only profitable way of explaining this is through a rational derivative that is anchored on axiological structures of meaning. As a consequence of this, etiology loses its vitality and is seen as nothing short of the objectification of tendencies which, having been over-determined, end up becoming immutable and unalterable. Yet, the immutability and inalterability of values – the primary source of 'ultimateness' – are ideal expressions of patterns of interlocking affinities, a paradoxical equation that is truly complex to unravel.

We will take but a sample. The immortal instinct is the expression of man's desire for self-perpetuation. One way he seeks to achieve this is not by the biological prolongation of life. Science here plays but a piteous role because exercises, healthy diets and new discoveries in biotechnology which seek to arrest the ageing process and extend lifespan are still subject to inescapable material mortality – but by attunement with the Godhead, a covenantal relationship that ensures an eternal life after earthly translation. Therefore, to die is to gain life anew, to incarnate into a divine state that is free from the scourges of material existence. Death, all manners and forms of death, is thus nothing but the justification of that immortal instinct, the highest demonstration of the ultimatum of value.

Do we then say that weeping, lamentations, gnashing of teeth and grieving during burial funeral rites are but cultural expressions – as a consequence of long sustained traditions and conventions? Hardly, not. Death, which achieves for man a permanent state of immortality, is rejected as a source of eternal life. Death wish in numerous cultures is an abomination. Death frights, narrow escapes, avoided accidents, close shaves, etc. are celebrated with spiritual outpouring of emotions in thanksgiving masses presided over by members of the theological and priestly class. Verses from sacred writings are quoted as a demonstration of God's love for his servant, a love which sees him shielding his creation from unwarranted harm. Yet no harm is unwarranted for harms incarnate a process – death – that will irresistibly be translated into that immortal wish. Forget the paradox of Lazarus' death, family grief and re-awakening, for that will open up a cultural vista that may be difficult for the consciousness of today's men to comprehend.

What, however, is obvious is that man is forever attracted

to the ultimate value of immortality and yet man readily negates the structure through which he will achieve his desired state. Man is always wishing and longing for transcendental union and bond with extraterrestrial forces, yet he is reluctant, profoundly reluctant, to sever his connection with the nature he sees and feels. It thus becomes abundantly clear that man's immortal instinct and the whole range of values he creates and conditions in justification of it is nothing but an expression of his cultural consciousness, an awareness of the expansive and extensive structure of reality and existence. In spite of their different realms of transfiguration, they remain products of culture and, as such, are organically dependent on the impulses that animate the terrestrial ordering and manifestation of nature. Such urgings are therefore only plausible on the terms set by nature and, to this extent, are limited by cultural conditionings which explode their pretensions as ultimate values.

Conventional wisdom has it that the atonement which follows a "narrow miss" is usually followed by the reformation of character and shift in value. The logic behind this pattern of reasoning is that divine protection from harm leads to a re-dedication of self to the Godhead via a passionate declaration of goodness till eternity.

However, the experience of people all over the world belies this delusive thinking. After the initial motions of re-conversion through rites of prayer and appearances at fellowships, individuals are wont to live their lives as in the old ways, believing in the efficacy of their affirming values, and the material rewards of their practical endeavours. I wonder how many corporate hounds or insider traders or highly prized prostitutes, or operators of business scams, or even petty thieves ever change their ways of life after a "narrow miss", and after the rite of atonement which a thanksgiving is.

Atonement is but a temporary loss of faith in the legitimacy of material life and the values it spawns. Its life-span is brittle for once the original danger is successfully disempowered, the pattern of affirmation and overdetermination remains unchanging. Atonement is an incidental longing for a lost communion; lost because the ultimate value it harbours – eternal life – is usually far removed from the immediate consciousness of mankind. To atone for one's misdeeds is to refrain from untoward conducts, yet like the Catholic confession, it exists as an empty ritual in relation to man's awareness of the possibilities inherent in his culture. His cultural expression is always a negation of the future materiality of atonement and this being so, he remains bound by and to the instant rewards that flow from his self-enhancing cultural performance.

Chapter 5

LITERARY VALUES

Here, we are not essentially concerned with the theory and process of literary production – Pierre Marchery has enlightened us sufficiently on that – nor are we going to investigate, in any detail, the relationship between "artistic truth" and the facts of life – Lucien Goldmann, Terry Eagleton and Raymond Williams, even over and beyond the structuralist, post-structuralist, deconstructionist, post-deconstructionist, modernist, postmodernist and reader-response technicians of our time, have more than instructed us on this matter. We shall be mainly concerned with literature as an incarnation of material life, as a form of cultural expression which, though appropriates to itself a unique form of affirmation of values, is organically interlinked with other existing life-forms.

A number of statements ought to be made at the onset. Literature is neither an imitation of life, its approximation in an imaginative way nor does it, through the elemental force of verisimilitude, seek a coherent identification with "real-life". The factor of mediation which is ascribed to the creative agent is but the concealment of material attitudes (consciousness also plays a part) inherent in the artist's predisposition towards the affirmation, over-determination and disempowerment of values. If objective intention is nothing but the mastery of mediated cultural reality, a literary production thus becomes the execution of cultural forces selected by the artist for approval or denunciation.

D.H. Lawrence's assumption that a literary work is only true within its time and place and untrue outside its time and place seeks to achieve a distance between culture and the products it incarnates. It separates, through this distance, nature against itself by appropriating a cultural facilitator (the literary artist) and the objective terms set by all manners of cultural facilitations (the literary product) outside their context of incarnation. The same applies, even to a higher degree, to the belief that art exists for its "de-humanized" and "de-humanizing" sake alone; a literary postulation that is nothing short of intellectual fancy, for the prime subject of art remains nature in its multi-faceted dimensions, including its cogent expressive formal requirement (language).

It is not just that literature can never manifest values in vacuum but that the space it creates for itself; that is, the cultural space created by the value-incarnating mediator is precisely the same space that is created by nature as a substance of material life, and nature in its expansive transcendence. This, of course, explains the close affinity between material life and literature of social realism, and transcendental life and heroic, epic, fabular, mythic, parabolic, liturgical, and transmagoric tales.

To search for the values which literature carries is to establish the fact, not the truth, that in spite of the capacious nature of the human mind, no writer can ever recognize reality beyond the limitations of his imagination. The elemental sources of imaginings, sensations and perceptions, of course, remain the substances of existing culture apprehended variously in primary experiencing, and in other forms of secondary experiencing. This Lukacian thesis is distinct from the assumed limitless capacity or competence of the essential literary reflector, the artistic image; a form of idealization of the legitimacy of all manners of expressive forms noticeable in the critical works of Roger Gaurady.

The production of literary values follows the same pattern as the production of other cultural values – through the process of individuation. Most theorists of orature miss this point, believing, as they do, that communal art is the earliest expression of artist consciousness, when in fact the collectivization or communalization of art is a form of an over-determined inheritance after the disempowerment of primordial values incarnated by individuals in history's earliest cradle. For it is through a successful affirmation of collective will over disparate autonomous values spawned by individuals with sovereign status, that there begins to emerge a corporate tendency in artistic consciousness.

Till date, the conflict of will in cultural expression still persists between artists who seek the validity of their individuated values and other artists who reflect, in a conformist sense, the prevailing cultural values of their time. There is no geometric line drawn in this, for creative individuality is one of the perquisites of true art; the zone of tension becomes clearer depending on the distance individual artists create between the values which are inconsistent with the prevailing cultural orthodoxy and those other values which are commonly tolerated, respected and even sanctified.

Thus, the dilemma which individuals face in the affirmation of values through which they seek to achieve relevance and recognition (all kinds of values and all kinds of recognitions are at work here – all authentic in themselves) when they are confronted with the facts of corporate cultural values already over-determined by state structures, either through willing association or through coercion, is the same kind of dilemma that literary artists face as they try to balance individual sensitivities and susceptibilities with the collective consciousness of their milieu. This may not readily appear so for art has, over the centuries, been somewhat separated from the material foundations of life, experience, reality and existence; a process, as we have already stated, which conceals and shields it from the tensions that material existing and experiencing generates.

Even at this, this separation is only noticeable in the so-called liberal societies, especially in the contemporary epoch, whose permissiveness and expansion of the legitimate zones of cultural conducts foreclose a systematic censure of the values which literary products incarnate. In less liberal states, like during the Stalinist rigidification of the tenets of Socialist Realism in the then Soviet Union, or in despotic authority structures in Africa, Middle East, and Asia, the values generated by literature are near totally aligned, and are made valid only on the terms determined by the cultural values incarnated by such prevailing "orthodoxies".

Writers are not regarded as dissidents and made to suffer for the "sin" of dissidence in some societies principally because they have a developed will to power (some do; while others may even be apolitical in terms of acquisition of political power, Salman Rushdie, for instance). The dissident status ascribed to writers has its foundation in the conflict between values. When the literary values in a writer's product challenge the legitimacy of an established cultural order, the struggle for affirmation which nature jealously seduces as its sole property, becomes a contest between individually determined will and the over-disempowering excesses of the cultural establishment. The restriction of the validity of a writer's cultural affirmation only to himself is considered a half measure for the product which he sells has a social reach; therefore, the de-affirmation of his expressed values, in aid of the sustenance of the monopolizing values of the cultural monolith, must be effectuated either by death, banishment, confinement or a censorship placed on the circulation of such a product with the values it carries.

In their purest form, certain literary values attract no

attention to themselves since their recognition and legitimacy as values are self-imbedded in cultural references prevailing in any given society. The same applies to all kinds of non-literary values whose signification as elements of cultural harmony is also derived from their "harmless" disposition. This is precisely why any consideration of literary values may in fact be structured along the basic lines demarcated by the operating collective cultural wills. To achieve this state of cognition will involve an understanding of the following, among other shaping cultural forces:

i. The nature of individually incarnated literary values in relation to the prevailing cultural values of a milieu;
ii. The distance literary artists create through the process of mediation, intervention, selection and creative individuality, between their individual cultural will and the communal cultural will they are part of;
iii. The nature of cultural affirmation existing in any given milieu; that is, the relationship between the cultural affirmation of the mass of the people and that of the ruling caste, and their standpoint on this; and
iv. The ability of literary artists to create a tension-free cultural climate through the reflection of cultural values in their original, autonomous, pure, harmless and non-individuated form.

This last point demands further clarification. Very many people assume that because love, anger, passion and all sorts of emotions are generally acknowledged cultural products, they escape the tension and distance which we declare always exist in any cultural environment, to the extent that their reflection in literary works require no manner of affirmation, over-determination and disempowerment with the resultant salutary or unsalutary consequences for the literary reflector. Such an assumption misses the cultural issue under contention.

Love for example, remains a harmless life-form to the extent that its cultural manifestation and literary reproduction are consistent with society's moral attitude towards it. This is why millions of romance novels and love poems flourish and are taken for granted, but not so, a literary work that reflects homosexual, lesbian, bi-sexual and incestuous love relationship between individuals in a society where such practices are not merely abhorred but are banned outrightly. The fate which some of D.H. Lawrence's novels suffered at their publication and the fate suffered by "underground" literature of Victorian England is still the fate suffered today by thousands of novels that are produced in a number of countries where the notion of love as a cultural value runs counter and achieves a concrete distance between love values incarnated by that society's individual members and which may be reflected in literary productions.

How about history as a source of literary values, one might ask. What threat does an ancient historical material pose to the over-determining instincts of a ruling caste to the degree that its incarnation in a literary work will entail censure for the literary artist? It is true that literary artists, sometimes, use concealed references, symbolic parallels, parables, fabular tales and ancient historical materials in the production of literary values in order to maintain the autonomous, legitimate status of the values they project. Other writers, moreover, indulge in historical and cultural escapism by either reflecting values whose historical sources are tolerated by the ruling caste, or through the distortion of such materials (attitudinizing) in order to accommodate an over-determined cultural climate they may even wish to attenuate as individuals through de-affirmation.

However this issue is approached, the fact remains that the cogency of historical consciousness is not time or space bound. History is a species of indeterminate cultural reality whose pristine incarnation is forever rendered valid and authentic by new experiences. Though man keeps on repeating the same historical blunders structured along the lines of distant tragedies, he is equally stubbornly insistent that he has learnt and mastered all learnable historical lessons. Man is thus frightened by the spectacle of history, seeing in the display of long forgotten follies a mockery of his present imperfect state. He is thus always in the search of historical allusions and parallels, particularly those that remind him that his fate is no different from the destiny of the tragic subjects he is a witness to.

In consideration of this, literary artists who deploy historical materials for the production of literary values may, indeed, expect no respite from society's dominant authority structures, like a director of *Macbeth* who presents the play as a birthday gift to a political usurper who assassinated the previous president to attain his present status, or a re-enactment of the Greek myth dealing with Paris' forceful elopement with Helen in a public performance organized in honour of a political leader who has just snatched his best friend's wife.

Because the fate of Macbeth and Paris is less than noble, such manner of incarnation of historical and mythic values in a literary context may even exaggerate the insensate passions of such an honoured guest who may, in fact, see the artist as a subversive element as Plato did with regard to poets in *The Republic*. Thus, the values which literature produces out of history achieve their state of respective affirmations, not on the terms dictated by those historical materials, but as end-products of existing historical and cultural attitudes.

Oftentimes, historical novels, plays and poems are ululated or denounced depending on the cultural forces at work at the moment of their creation. Others are, in fact, reactions to perceived distortions of historical and cultural sources from where they are derived, like when Chinua Achebe stated that one of his objective intentions in writing *Things Fall Apart* is to render to his people an authentic picture of their historical being and becoming as against its vulgarization by Joyce Cary in *Mister Johnson*. Other African writers in fact discovered their latent artistic creativity on reading Joseph Conrad's *Heart of Darkness* which they considered a racially disempowering novel and produced literary works that constitute a refutation of his affirming cultural will.

I recall too Ngugi wa Thiong'o's account of the process whereby his novel, *Matigari,* ended up in exile; a process which began with the rumours that a historical subject, called *Matigari,* has been sighted in the mountains demanding justice and asking embarrassing questions, and a trail that led to the discovery that Matigari is indeed a character in a novel, whereupon Kenyan authorities not only placed a ban on its further reprinting but also caused to be removed and burnt all existing copies in bookstores. At other times, too, certain historical periods become a taboo subject in some less liberal societies, no matter the angle of reflection, as is the case in a number of despotic outfits in Africa, Middle East and some parts of Asia.

What, then, are the constitutive elements of literary values? As we stressed in chapter five, the gift of instinctual conduct nourished over time out of which the illuminating consciousness of literary artists and those others we call masters of consciousness derive, is structured along the same thesis of autonomy of values, affirmation of values, over-determination of values and the disempowerment of values just as other cultural values are. The pursuit of knowledge in literature here becomes the determination of creative strategies through which literary artists incarnate values in their work, their loyalty or fidelity to the autonomous property of values – all values – and the cultural restrictions which lead either to over-determination or disempowerment of values in literary productions.

Any excursion into history and myth will reveal that the earliest forms of literature incarnate values based on cultural transcendence. Transcendental consciousness thus, lies at the root of man's earliest literary imagination not as a specific response to an incomprehensible cosmos, but as an art of over-determination. Why is this always so? We have seen the methods of transition whereby material values in their purest, autonomous form undergo systematic distortion from the point of individuated existence, to social contractual affirmation and, finally, to transcendental over-determination.

Therefore, the disempowerment of individuated values by an aggressive cultural communion reaches a point in which that material communion loses its legitimacy to cultural transcendence. Man as a social organizer and in the earliest type of binding social contracts he establishes for himself, always over-projects his cultural reach in favour of those primordial life and value forms which his consciousness of material nature could not objectively perceive. He declares his dependence, together with other members of his community, not to the cultural values that ensure his material affirmation on earth, but to externalized and distantiated transcendental values which he regards as being ultimate in nature, character and substance. The process of distantiation is thus a cultural organism whereby social terms of reference are not complete in themselves without the participation and determination of extra-terrestrial forces.

We see this illustrated in virtually all national literatures where the production of literary values is undertaken or achieved in response to the specificities of those elements of cultural transcendence. We will illustrate with just a few examples.

Earliest Greek literature is an intermixture of history and cultural transcendence expressed in the capacious competence of myth and ritual as providers of clues to the riddle of existence and the substance of universal destiny. The values this literature embodies, in spite of its extensive historical reach and authenticity as Marx correctly demonstrated, are values whose cultural conditioning stems from the sanctification of unalterable transcendental laws. Whether in the fables of Aesop or the mythic tragedies of Sisyphus and Narcissus; whether in the heroism of Heracles,

Jason, Icarus and Daedalus or in the *Iliad and Odyssey* of Homer, whereupon the respective destinies of Achilles, Hector, Aeneas, Patroculus, Paris, etc are seen as the universal dependence of man on the higher ordering of cultural reality; or in the plays of Aeschylus, Sophocles and Euripides; the elements of cultural transcendence, ultimate values and unalterable laws pervade the entire literary-cultural spectrum.

Achilles, for example, was very conscious of the substance of this transcendental conditioning for he deliberately elected to achieve a short and sharp heroic immortality – via material translation – on the plains of Troy than live to a grand, unremembered old age as the master of the Myrmidons of Phthia in Thessaly. Not so Sarpedon whose fate was nearly altered without his knowledge through the emotive intervention of his divine father, Zeus, but for the gentle rebuttal of Hera who alerted her brother and husband about the sanctioned immutability of divine order and the disastrous consequence of such a reversal of fortune on the cultural coherence of the universe.

For Gerrymanders, the destined journey to immortality involved no material transition for being the most beautiful youth in the world at his time, he was kidnapped by the gods because of his looks to become Zeus' cupbearer and thus forgathered with the gods in eternity. But for Ajax, the son of Telamon, and the King of Salamis, his process of non-material transfiguration was a most painful one. Having lost out to Odysseus in the contest for Achilles' divine armour, he went mad with shame and committed suicide, a source of cultural incoherence for Odysseus met his soul, as resentful as ever, in Hades during his wonderings after the sacking of Troy.

For the Greek literary masters, heroic recounters and mythic poets, the attributions of immortality do not derive only from man's dependence on fate or the intermixure of earthly blood with its divine counterpart (ichor) but also essentially from the inherent structure of cultural coherence which an established world order guarantees. Tragic poetry, for instance, is not enacted for the task of instruction alone, for through it is maintained both the awareness of truth rendered transcendentally comprehensible and the expectation that the fulfilment of destiny is virtually consistent with the attainment of immortality.

Oedipus was unaware of his earthly inheritance, yet his search for truth and justification which pushed him to the brink of knowing, a destructive occult zone of oracular consciousness, became a cultural organism whereby his earthly *peripetiea* necessarily presaged his transfiguration into a world of non-material culture. Both the artist and his subject, in this instance, and in other classical Greek instances, were all unable to incarnate or produce values with sovereign or autonomous will. Thus, lacking the element of individuation and affirmation through cultural conflict, such values, at their immediate manifestation in literary and mythic works, become instantaneously transcendental in nature and orientation.

Thus, while it may be justified to argue that classical Greek literature (classical Roman literature is another example) is the systematization and legitimization of a transcendental cultural ideology – a system in which man is but a pawn in a cosmic chess game – under which values are incarnated or produced in justification of man's subservience to extra-terrestrial forces; and in which tragedy becomes nothing but a structure of illumination about the capacious character of nature in transcendence, it may still be very proper to pursue a course of reflection that separates this transcendental culture from man's creative will.

To do this may entail a deliberate blocking of part of our cognitive resources, in order to see the attributions of heroism, honour, gallantry, betrayal, love, ecstasy and death as values which exist in themselves, and which provide guidance to the conduct of the affairs of people. It is only on this basis that any examination of these literary values could be undertaken out of which would emerge for the contemporary man, an apprehension of their patterns of affirmation, over-determination and disempowerment via the cultural distance that we have perceptually achieved or created.

The classical Greek example holds well with regard to the mythic narrations and ritual performances of other cultural entities in the world. In Africa, India, and China, to name but a few such cultural milieu, the issue is not essentially the narrative and formal limitations of myth as literature or the dramatic limitations of ritual as artistic performance (this is a primary aesthetic matter), but in locating the non-individualized (as against the determinate individualization of Greek literature) values such myths and rituals incarnate under the context of a pervasive transcendental cultural consciousness.

Such myths and rituals celebrate a culture in infinite transition from quantity to quantity, form to form and from substance to substance in a regulated cosmic order. They are thus values which not only exonerate man (in a collective sense) from the substance of universal destiny, but also declare for themselves their integral affinity with the ascribed cultural coherence of the world based on the perquisites of those extraterrestrial entities.

Here again, the values of valour, honour, heroism, treachery and love may be studied for the sake of the cultural and social properties they harbour and which may be beneficial for today's affirmations, independent of their thorough dependence on culture-in-transcendence through which they are legitimated. Here, also, we pursue this course of cultural dialogue, mindful of the fact that to do so would mean once more, the tailoring of a partially selective perceptual paradigm based on the distance we declare does exist between the material incarnation of values and its determination by transcendental will.

In Western literature, for instance, we may glide over the undeveloped nature of literary values in the middle period as a consequence of the illumination of universal cultural meaning based essentially on the determinants of a transcendental Christian ethical system which was the propulsive rationalization and moral enthusiasm of the Holy Roman Empire (Chaucer and Bunyan suffered the same cultural fate as did the producers of miracle and morality plays like *Everyman*). The recycling of such transcendental cultural values as eternal life, penitence, divine knowledge through travails, spiritual labour and sacrifice, penance, repentance, atonement of sins, etc in this literature appears primitive to the values incarnated by the literature of renaissance and enlightenment.

We do this because, over and beyond the limitations of classical literature, we are dealing, during the middle period, with a literature that was thoroughly unaware of itself as a distinct form of cultural expression; a literature that was totally interlocked (in its sheer dependence), with extra-literary cultural forces; and a literature whose mode of incarnating values totally dispensed with the principles of production through individuation, collective affirmation through social contract and over-determination and disempowerment through cultural conflict.

The literary instincts of the renaissance age found an expression in the paradigms of cultural coherence and paradoxes of cultural discontinuities. On the one hand, renaissance literature was a form of cultural illumination; that is, the freedom of intellect and the rediscovery of man's constant search for justification through the affirmation of values. This spirit which defined the literary productions of neoclassical artists created the necessary distance between the stifling medieval religious rigidification of existence and the age of change which science and human intellect heralded.

The celebration of heroism, honour and betrayal remained the irresistible foundation of renaissance literary consciousness, with the process of creative distantiation necessitating the invalidation of the earlier assumptions of cultural transcendence. The values which this literature purveyed, with the possible exception of the recreated myth of Faustus in the hands of both Marlowe, and subsequently Goethe, were values whose incarnation was dependent on material force; whose affirmation became an exercise of individual will; whose over-determination was deep-rooted in cultural conflict; and whose disempowerment only required the triumphal presence of other material values.

With the recession of God and the other divinities to the background of cultural imagination man became foregrounded as an individuated and individuating cultural force, with the consequence that the cognition and perception of values no longer necessitated any negotiation with other pre-determining terms of reference outside the realm of material culture, and nature as a concrete substance. Honour, heroism, ambition and loyalty became no longer the ideal expression of a well-regulated, predestined cultural charter, but cultural imperatives whose legitimacy and authenticity were principally dependent on the acts and conducts of men.

On the other hand, renaissance literary values became seduced by the cultural and social formalism of the age; by the interlocking of such values with the accepted cultural attitudes of the time; and by the pre-determination of the accentuation and enhancement of values on the systematized controlling cultural and moral paradigms spawned by the ruling establishments. The implication of this is that while the invalidity of cultural transcendence was virtually taken for granted, the behaviour of values became dependent, like in the case of Edward de Vere, who wrote the Shakespearian works, on the cultural and moral assumptions of an aristocratic elite.

The autonomy and affirmation of values, with particular reference to the Earl's works, were no longer conditioned by the process of legitimation through individuation but by a willing subscription to the cultural and moral world order of his age. The harm this did to culture, and to literature as a form of cultural expression, is that such values, say heroism, could no longer be separated and studied as autonomous values, but must be perceived from the pre-determined cultural attitudes, not of the mass of the people in their specific individualities, but as a statement of the instincts of the prevailing cultural orthodoxy.

Here, then, we are confronted with an age which freed man's cultural instincts from the bonds of transcendental loyalty; which fed those instincts with a multiplicity of cultural nuances and legitimate imperatives; which broke down the barriers that separated all manners of cultural dialogues; which, through creative distantiation and artistic mediation, extended man's apprehension of the expansive cultural tensions, uncertainties and incompleteness of an organic universe that is always eager to absorb and adapt to the needs of new cultural meanings and moral foundations; and yet, an age of cultural formalism and social regimentation, which wreaked as much havoc on the autonomous incarnation and affirmation of values as did the Middle Period it challenged, invalidated and supplanted.

While the renaissance age was caught in the trap set by cultural tradition and change and "managed" to impose cultural order on the chaos of existence after the image of an accepted cultural orthodoxy, the age of enlightenment dispensed with the element of cultural production of value as an end result of the prerogatives of any prescribed cultural orthodoxy. It was to reason, dialogue and systematized values that it turned to for inspiration, and in the hands of the French masters like Voltaire, Rousseau and Robespierre, this cultural organism became virtually channelled in the service of nihilistic causes.

The energy of the age of enlightenment derived from the absence of cultural attitudinizing and moral reflection (read moral as the will of a dominant cultural monolith); in short, a strategy of cultural discord that was ultimately designed to restore to values their autonomy as existing life-forms and authority as valid forms of cultural expression. In pursuit of these goals, the literary values of the enlightenment, whether in the plays of Moliere and Ibsen, or in the philosophic treatises of Voltaire and Rousseau, were values whose meaningfulness is basically enhanced at their moment of incarnation and whose authenticity is already self-ascribed as a consequence of their autonomous generation.

There was, thus, little doubt that such values as liberty, egalitarianism, equality of all forms of human brotherhood and fraternity, the danger of over-determined cultural and social conducts and the need to redefine, re-categorize and re-typologize moral and cultural beliefs became not only its signature but laid the ground for the subsequent collapse of moral and cultural orthodoxies at the political level (read the French Revolution of 1789 as just one instance of this collapse).

Here, too, we are almost certain that the worship of freedom and moral liberty is a form of over-determination of value, meaning that the excess of this during the age was no longer a mere challenge to the cultural assumptions of the ruling caste but another form of over-assertion of values. This is precisely so because with the disempowerment of the prevailing cultural attitudes of the age, those ascendant values which only sought for recognition through affirmation inexorably became over-determined upon successful legitimation, and in the condition of their declared and accepted triumphal presence. This tendency, however, is evidence of a higher cultural consciousness, for values must at all times draw their strengths and weaknesses in the context of interaction; the infinite orientation of this conflictual pattern of interaction (a Marxian thesis) is the concrete engine on which cultural transition and cultural succession are based.

The advanced development of material forces and the tensions this created for cultural coherence separated the 19th century from other preceding historical epochs. Whether in the works of Zola, Balzac, Stendhal, the Goncourt brothers, etc (France) or in the works of Gogol, Turgenev, Dostoyevsky, Lermontov, Tolstoy, etc (Russia) or in the works of Dickens, Elliot, Thackary, Walter Scott, Arnold, etc

(England), the tendency towards the dissociation of cultural sensibility received decisive impetus from complex patterns of social contradictions which such a material age underlaid. In spite of the mediation strategies such writers adopted, and their remarkable illuminating gift of creative individuality, the cultural message that came across was always often programmatic and tendentious.

Whether in the area of social realism or in the assessment of psychological conditioning of individuals caught between personal aspirations and attainments and the prevailing collective social and cultural sanctions, 19th century literary instincts exaggerated the necessity of over-determination of values as against the free play of autonomous cultural life-forms. Themes relating to poverty, over-crowding, unemployment, abuse of women and the deprived, child labour, the haunting images of alcoholics, "fallen" women, and mentally disabled people, who constitute the class of the insulted, abused and injured, became products of selective and subjective imagination which in turn failed to create a distance between what is culturally valid and what should be culturally legitimate.

What is conveniently brushed aside – this achieves no literary demonstration – is that the state of any cultural value at any historical epoch is a consequence of conflict between autonomous life-forms, and that the cultural image of the age which the writers found distasteful was created by a long period of cultural continuity and transition from quantity into quantity. The 19th century was, thus, an age in which writers, in their creative efforts to disempower existing values through the restoration of invalidated life-forms to their original state of autonomy, in turn over-determined the cultural images they accepted as rational and logical at the expense of values which have already declared their triumphal presence.

The end-result of this literature is that apart from providing cogent illumination regarding existing social and psychological states of being, it led to the sustenance of an unchanging cultural tradition that transfigured the individuation of values at their state of incarnation from their primary context of cultural reference to a state in which values are made to harbour, not their constant autonomous instincts, but the over-determining instincts of their literary producers.

This systematic consolidation of ideal cultural expressions that are uprooted from their existing cultural sources and rendered as valid cultural organisms in spite of their state of legitimacy or otherwise, were to be seen, not only in the works of the producers already named, but also in the works of Mark Twain, the American transcendentalists, Stephen Crane, etc, and in virtually all the literary productions of the age as a whole as any worthwhile research will illuminate.

The 20th century literary milieu is defined by cultural dissonance, incoherence and chaos. The search for coherence, order and association became a relentless one; as relentless as those forces that redefined the objective meaning of cultural freedom. The beauty of that century is that it harboured within its cultural tradition an enormous quantity of autonomous cultural forces that invalidated any attempt at erecting a cultural or literary monolith: the First and Second World Wars, Hitlerism, the Russian Revolution of 1917, the struggle of colonial dependencies for statehood and national sovereignty, the sexual revolution, feminism, the rise of new age cultural nihilism and narcissism, the culture of unbelief, mutations in organized religion, new cultic consciousness, universalizing of oriental mysticism, etc.

The kaleidoscopic pattern of the century's cultural consciousness was thus nothing but a continuing struggle between conflicting life-forms. Out of this struggle is derived the highest demonstration of mankind's cultural and literary liberty. Literary individuation which was temporarily subverted by the Stalinist rigidification of the tenets of Socialist Realism remained the primary source for the incarnation of values, to the extent that their autonomy, affirmation, over-determination and over-empowerment virtually lacked credibility beyond the realized cognitive consciousness of the literary producers.

The implication of this for cultural continuity is that the succession from one valid cultural value to another and the transition, in quantity and quality, from life-forms to life-forms no longer owed any pre-determination to a coherently organized cultural system. The values this literary tradition spawned, including the tradition of cultural resistance and national affirmation in Africa, Asia, Middle East and Latin America are values which seek their meaning, relevance and significance outside the specificities of a universally accepted cultural organism. They are values which depend almost solely on localized cultural particulars for sanction, and values which successfully hide their individuated process of incarnation from the excessive demands of embattled cultural orthodoxies via creative mediation and artistic distantiation. Even when these values are compelled to behave after a regulated cultural pattern, they still testify to the immanence of cultural dissociation and incoherence by the way of convoluted experiments in form and language.

In essence, literary values are values produced from life, and life in itself is a rendition in non-formal terms of all manners of cultural diversities. Literature, like other cultural products, if it must aid the pursuit of cultural liberty, must recognize, from the onset, the autonomous incarnation of all life-forms, and must investigate, not for the sake of propaganda, but in the pursuit of that liberty, the patterns new cultural particulars evolve out of the tradition of cultural conflict and struggle. To achieve this end is to reject the over-determined cultural nuances of the milieu as adequate evidence of their legitimacy, and to insist that the recognition of the existence of value, any value, at a determinate cultural epoch is in itself enough justification of its autonomy, whether indeed it is sufficiently asserted, over-affirmed or relatively disempowered by existing cultural attitudes.

Chapter 6

THE ELYSIAN FIELDS AND THE QUEST FOR ETERNAL BLISS

Charles Mills Gayley, editing Bulfinch's *Age of Fable*, an old book that I still find more than useful given the chaos in the contemporary intellectual assessment of the origin and meaning of culture, supplies the mythic mode of cultural apprehension; mode in that the underlying substratum of the mythic imagination has very minimal mythic implication. Like all cultural assumptions, the world of myth is an intermixture of various layers of determinations. Ultimately, the correlating ingredients of determinations are basically transformed, first into affirmations, and subsequently into reinventions. The idea of cultural continuum is based on this causal logic; both the continuum ascribed to the apprehension of material cultural as an organic index of social interrelationships, and the continuum which weaves a web around cultural materiality and cultural transcendence.

The classical mythic world owes cultural affinity to a delusive technological age and yet successfully contradicts it on a number of salient points. The Olympian region was the *sanctus sanctorum* of cultural forces who wear the skein of undiluted immortality in spite of their autochthonous heritage. The visible material world was the **Upper Air** inhabited by men, beasts, and other materially apprehensible nature while **Hades** created for itself a multiplicity of cultural sub-regions chief among which were **The Elysian Fields**, the **Infernal Regions**, and the **Valley of Oblivion**. Determinate and indeterminate crossovers were allowed, making a neat cultural separation a task beyond the grasp of average intelligence.

The world of myth, if it could be called that, was decisively unpretentious in its rendition of cultural accounts with its overwhelming dependence on an injunctious ethical logic that thoroughly disempowers all values not legitimated within its inherently self-regulating connectedness. The fact of pre-determination of values was taken for granted; so also was the somewhat irascible application of the logic of over-determination wherein derived the cultural communion that made for coherence, binding conducts and the continuity that was built into the cultural system.

Yet, in the age of super conductivity, the internet and the World Wide Web, space probes and all manners of technological advertisements, the terror of the unknown still weighs man down as never before in all the history of his material incarnation over the preceding millennia. High Olympus still stands as an embodiment of cultural transcendence, minus the minor adjustment from a polytheistic ethos into a monotheistic imagination. The battle for the possession of material nature as in the near infinitude of the flora and fauna potentials of the world's rain forests (read the Amazon) continues with the same frenzy as in the age of myth. Other manners of cultural crossover occur at the material plane as the reluctance to shed the stifling deceit of "orthodox practices" is increasingly giving way to the enthusiastic reassessment of the potentials and benefits of herbs, barks of trees and roots as curative therapies of new diseases and old maladies.

The Elysian Fields is nothing but an incarnation of a new paradise, a new state of blessedness, with new human angels performing the task of the ageless Charon who ferried bodied and disembodied entities over the ever-flowing and ever-busy purgatory river of fate to be deposited on the opposite shore, from where they will proceed to the different regions of cultural transcendence depending on how well they lived their lives in the world of material culture. Virtually all modern religions accept these cultural images and demarcations and, to this extent, is ascertained the certainty of cultural stagnation and arrested consciousness between the tender roots of a mythic era and the over-bloated pretensions of the current age.

At the root of mankind's cultural dilemma remains the quest for immortality and eternal bliss which only a defined state of conscious blessedness can provide. To tackle this cultural embarrassment, we take recourse in Bullfinch and Gayley.

The Elysian Fields:

> The Sibyl now warned Aeneas that it was time to turn from these melancholy regions and seek the city of the blessed. They passed through a middle track of darkness and came upon Elysian Fields, the groves where the happy reside. They breathed a freer air, and saw all objects clothed in a purple light. The region had a sun and stars of its own. The inhabitants were enjoying themselves in various ways, some in sports on the grassy turf, in games of strength or skill, others dancing or singing. Orpheus struck the chords of his lyre, and called for the ravishing sounds. Here Aeneas saw the founders of the Trojan state, great-hearted heroes who lived in happier times. He gazed with admiration on the war chariots and glittering arms now reposing in disuse. Spears stood fixed in the ground and the horses, unharnessed, roamed over the plain ... He saw another group

feasting, and listening to the strains of music. They were in a laurel grove, whence the great river Po has its origin, and flows out among men, wherein dwelt those who fell by wounds received in their country's cause, holy priests also and poets who have uttered thoughts worthy of Apollo, and others who have contributed to cheer and adorn life by their discoveries in the useful arts, and have made their memory blessed by rendering services to mankind. They wear snow - white fillets about their brows. (Gayle, *Classic Myths in English Literature,* p. 35.)

The Elysian Fields is a refutation of the originality of the concept and vision of Eden. What is at play is that multiple historical and cultural traditions incarnate this vision of eternal blessedness based on the specific determinations of each milieu and ethnic sensibility. The precedence of one cultural vision over the other in the scale of originality is not even imperative here; the seduction of the idea of infinite bliss is more of a philosophical puzzle than an anthropological or ethnographic one. The real tragedy of modern culture is the assumption that man can and will attain a state of blessedness on earth and through that effectuate the importation of incarnated images of cultural transcendence into the world of material culture.

The very idea of modern civilization, at its most aggressive realm of techno-cultural advancement, is a human society run by competent men in government, business and bureaucracy; of leisure, sports, games and entertainment; of attainable health and physical fitness; of peace, and human rights observances; and of an interdependent community of free nations bound together by instant communication, shared cultural values, and diverse, though correlating ethical principles. Though this union, expressed in the imperfect assembly which the UN still is, is yet to fully master its ascribed affirmative possibilities, it remains the sovereign goal of today's leaders in government and organized religion.

There is little doubt that man's search for immortality and a state of blessedness begins here on earth given his interstellar vision and desire to conquer outer space. Such cultural incursions which disempower other entities not considered animate are hoped to create the necessary channels, and connecting links between mankind's cultural illumination in a universe he possesses and the extraterrestrial region he desires to dwell in.

Even today, the agenda of all governments – the question of classification is an absurd moral category – is the determination of necessary and not so necessary needs, the affirmation of those needs, and the securing for their citizens a certain state of blessedness through the disempowerment of cultural, material and human impediments. To secure this state of bliss is to create an earthly Elysian Fields, and in so doing to separate the cultural parameters of such a perfectly functioning Upper Air from the terror of the Infernal Regions and the sonambulance of the Valley of Oblivion.

In attempting to create this cultural distance, modern man, through his governments, hopes to free the earth from beings who inhabit the two dangerous regions of the underworld: through the judicial and penal system, other forms of confinement, execution of "criminals", "murderers" and violators of the envisaged State of Bliss, and the deployment of civil and not so civil security agencies to make the attainment of this cultural state a realistic goal.

Yet, in spite of all manners of cultural manoeuvres, the search for the Elysian Fields on earth becomes trapped in a pseudo-mythic nightmare for while the mythic accounts of the separation of the cultural realm into regions of glory and damnation was a product of an ideal consciousness which subsisted on cultural suppositions (on the basis of the particular context of the production of values and their imaginative transformation from a material plane into a transcendental axis), the modern age dispenses with this conscious illusion and declares that the failure of such classical realization is a product of the age of innocence which civilization has more than redressed.

This cultural pitfall has led to the systematic implantation of the scourges of the Infernal Regions (a materially non-existent entity) into a materially existing universe: the data on this are available at the UN headquarters in New York and Geneva, ranging from the casualties of wars in the past 73 years, child labour, child soldiers and child abuse, abuse of women, poverty, malnutrition, refugee problems, state terrorism and other crimes against humanity, including the millions who die yearly from hunger and diseases; to the unprecedented assault on the environment that has made elnino, Tsunami, greenhouse effect, global warming, the depletion of the ozone layer and the thawing of the Antarctic and Arctic ice belt a grim reality of the current age.

Here then, we witness a cultural descent from the search for blessed immortality and a state of bliss on earth to the realm of transcendental cultural damnation imaginatively reconstructed during the classical age. Very few people can deny that the state of humanity today is a material incarnation of the Infernal Regions of hell, repeatedly borrowed by latter-day religious persuasions and frighteningly reproduced by James Joyce in his Daedallian quest for transcendental consciousness through epiphanic illumination in *A Portrait of an Artist as a Young Man*. Here, then, is the Infernal Regions providing, as it does, a ready comparison with the modern techniques of affirmation and over-determination by world institutions at the head of this search for blessedness:

The Infernal Regions:

> Before they descended the threshold of hell they passed through a group of beings who are enumerated as Grief's and Avenging Cares, Pale Diseases, and Melancholy Age, fear and hunger that

tempt to crime, toil, poverty and death, forms horrible to view. The Furies spread their couches there, and Discord, whose hair was of uppers tied up with a bloody fillet. Here also were the monsters, Briareus, with his hundred arms, Hydra-hissing, and Chimaeras breathing fire. They then came to the black river Cocytus, where they found the ferryman, Charon, old and squalid, but strong and vigorous, who was receiving passengers of all kinds into his boat, stout hearted heroes, boys and unmarried girls, as numerous as the leaves that fall at autumn ... They stood pressing for a passage and longing to touch the opposite shore. But the stern ferryman took in only such as he chose, driving the rest back.[2]

The first sound that struck their ears was the wailing of young children, who had died on the threshold of life, and near to these were they who had perished under false charges. The next class was those who had died by their own hands, hating life and seeking refuge in death. Next were situated the regions of sadness, divided off into retired paths, leading through groves of mettle. Here roamed those who had fell victims to unrequited love, not freed from pain even in death itself.

They next came to a place where the road divided, the one leading to Elysium, the other to the Regions of the Condemned. Before him (Aeneas) was the gate of adamant that neither gods nor men can break through. An iron tower stood by the gate, on which

---

[2] According to classical myth, only those who have had due burial rites are permitted to board Charon's boat. The unburied must remain at the other side of the shore till such rites are performed. Check: Patroclus urging Achilles to bury him as quickly as he could, and the agony of King Priam of Troy not so much that Hector was slain by Achilles but that he had not received his due burial rites.

Tisiphone, the avenging fury, kept guard. From the city were heard groans, and the sounds of the scourge, the creaking of iron, and the clanking of chains ...

Aeneas saw groups seated at tables, loaded with dainties, while nearby stood a fury that snatched away the viands from their lips as fast as they prepared to taste them. Others beheld suspended over their heads huge rocks, threatening to fall, keeping them in a state of constant alarm. These were they who had hated their brothers, or struck their parents, or defrauded their friends, who trusted them, or who, having grown rich, kept their money to themselves, and gave no share to others; the last being the most numerous class. Here also were those who had violated the marriage vow, or fought in a bad cause, or failed in fidelity to their employers. Here was one who had sold his country for gold, another who perverted the laws, making them say one thing today and another tomorrow.

Ixion was there, fastened to the circumference of a wheel ceaselessly revolving and Sisyphus, whose task was to roll a huge stone up a hill top, but when the steep was well-nigh gained, the rock repulsed by some sudden force, rushed again headlong down the plain. Again, he toiled at it, while the sweat bathed all his weary limbs, but all to no effect. There was Tantalus, who stood in a pool, his chin level with the water, yet he was parched with thirst, and found nothing to assuage it, for when he bowed his hoary head eager to quaff, the water fled away, leaving the ground at his feet dry. Tall trees, laden with fruits, stooped their heads to him, pears, pomegranates, apples, and luscious figs; but when, with a sudden grasp, he tried to seize them; winds whirled them high above his reach.
(*Classic Myths in English Literature*, pp. 345-350.)

Ixion, Sisyphus, Tantalus and the other victims of a mythic universe whose ethical aura is defined by the absence of the pre-determination, determination and affirmation of free will were bound to the festering scourges of the Infernal Regions as a lesson to man whose own cultural product – the immortal pantheon – in turn established for him unattainable cultural and moral values that are transcendental in nature, but which he readily and not so readily accepted through binding cultural contracts of varied interrelationships. Sisyphus in particular has been resurrected in the modern age not so much by Albert Camus (The Myth of Sisyphus) and even not so much by the other existentialist masters like Malroux, Gide and Genet, but by the very character, structure and content of universal cultural connections.

The acceptance of the Sisyphean myth as a factor in mankind's contemporary cultural fate shares very little in common with the very idea of existentialist terror, absurd consciousness or the laden abominations of humanity; its main, essential cultural derivative is that the insistent, perpetual search for a state of blessedness has inexorably led to tragic cultural omissions that have transported, translated and transformed Sisyphus from his mythic, transcendental moorings into an identifiable material cultural energy in the modern age.

While it may require a Talmudic-like commentary to explicate the complex morphology and typology of the Infernal Regions, the element of cultural dissonance, or, rather the dissociation of sensibility that separates that mythic world from current cultural trends is easy to discern. For while most of the inhabitants of the Infernal Regions ran 'foul' of existing, transcendentally imposed moral codes, and were punished for so doing (another case of the non-originality of the incarnation of hell in modern religion), the earth as an Infernal Region owes its own brand of contradictions to the fact that most of today's victims of injustice are dehumanized on the basis of the over-determination of values materially incarnated.

From the Holocaust to Bosnia and Somalia; and from Rwanda to Burundi, the Infernal Regions of the world are populated by "innocents" who share no other aspiration in life apart from their desire to affirm the most basic level of humanity. Here again, we see the search for a state of blessedness leading in two directions: one, the corruption of a transcendental cultural principle into a determinate material category through the transfiguration of an ethical-mythic imagination into contemporary cultural reality; and two, the embarrassing descent into the state of cultural damnation through the sheer application of the fundamental derivative instrument of attaining the state of blessedness: disempowerment of values via the over-determination of a constricted triumphal cultural ethos.

Here again, a tension exists in the apprehension of the characteristics of today's cultural reality. The disallowance of the materiality of Olympus in favour of the immediacy of the Upper Air may well lead to the disallowance of the image of the Infernal Regions in favour of a moderated version of the Elysian Fields as the defining idiom of the modern age. The resolution of this tension involves an altogether different kind of cultural crossover. If humanity as it presently is today, is neither an Olympus, the Upper Air, the Elysian Fields nor the Infernal Regions, then what is it?

Such a cultural crossover seeks a certain degree of harnessing of cultural variables and suppositions, some autonomously incarnated and others as by-products of a long history of over-determination of values. If humanity is neither of these entities, it then must stand as the Valley of Oblivion, an occult zone of half-light and half-darkness, where all manners of cultural indeterminations are readily found. I find this characterization pertinently intriguing and suspect strongly that it will yield significant illumination in comprehending man's quest for eternal bliss.

The Valley of Oblivion is a transitional realm of cultural incarnation, reincarnation, mediation and reinvention. The specificities of these dependent cultural variables pertain to:

1. The supremacy of cultural transcendence over material culture in the production of values and other cultural entities within the organizing matrix of a coherent mythic imagination;
2. The transmutation of cultural types, including human agents, into new cultural images after a process of purgation; and
3. The re-orientation of cultural imperatives in a cyclic pattern that envisages the attainment of a desired state of unity between cultural materiality and cultural transcendence.

The Valley of Oblivion is thus a mythic-cultural clearing house in which allowance, dependent as it were on an obligatory cultural transcendence, is given to the affirmation of values, the over-determination of values and the disempowerment of values, in such a way as to make the achievement of cosmic balance possible. While the Valley of Oblivion is not necessarily the attenuation of the State of Blessedness, it does not **directly** and **instantly** aid the quest for eternal bliss. It remains, as we have already declared it to be, an occult zone of cultural indetermination, of sober reflection, and a realistic evaluation of the state of humanity.

But, of course, its primary significance is the deliberate and, sometimes, half-conscious subsumption of the primacy of cultural materiality to the enigmatic aura of cultural transcendence by a classical imagination which was apprehensive about the scope and dimension of nature. Such mythic accounts, including the relationship between the Valley of Oblivion and the Elysian Fields, which lie between the terror junctions of the Infernal Regions, are culturally nonsensical in that they remain the product of human imagination. It is at this stage that myth ceases to exist as an autotelic cultural entity and becomes the rendition, in non-material particulars, of the cultural forces which have been worked into human civilization.

In the contemporary age, the Valley of Oblivion should be seen as neither the elixir for cultural self-resurrection nor a catalyst for cultural amnesia. Its purpose is to seduce man out of a relentless, burdensome and, ultimately, destructive search for the ideal state. It should serve as a warning to those who have already proclaimed the end of all major cultural processes (Fukuyama) and those who demarcate an age from another based on what they consider quantum leaps in historical occurrences (John Lukacs).

While all polities seek and most often secure their legitimacy in the attainment of the ideals of governance with mass sanction, the excesses of statehood create a dissonance between such claims and the true state of humanity. In advanced liberal societies where the seduction of the search of eternal bliss is at its most exaggerated level, the pattern of cultural conducts reveals two disturbing scenarios; a descent into excessive hedonism and the compulsive acquisition of psychotic mentality which is manifest in a horrendous debasement of human dignity; anti-cultural sexual revolt, serial killings and sexual abuse, organized and individual crimes, orgiastic mass violence, social dislocations, cultural life as theatre and circus carnival and the imperialist exploitation, plunder and war of aggression against weaker, culturally disempowered peoples and entities.

In the so-called less developed polities, the search for the eternal state of bliss commences at the elementary level of human bestiality: detention and murder of political opponents, deliberately engineered regime of genocide, fratricidal warfares, hunger, poverty, and malnutrition, to the extent that the daily count of corpses in thousands and millions becomes a routine bureaucratic task. These excesses were demonstrated in Cambodia under Pol Pot, between 1975 and 1979 and Somalia, Rwanda and Burundi between 1991 and 1996.

The search for Ultimate Blessedness by the so-called developed societies has led to the hysteria over the preservation of endangered species (birds, beasts and plants); a responsibility which is obsessively cultivated by well-funded and well-endowed foundations not withstanding that if 20% of such funds are channelled into humane causes, there will be a tremendous reduction of hunger, poverty and malnutrition worldwide. In the developing states, the task of social engineering leads to a compulsive acquisition of weapons of war, the value of which is capable of wiping out all man-made and environmental/ ecological disasters. Yet, in each case the design of such cultural promoters is the attainment of a state of bliss which an envisaged and sought after Elysium will provide and guarantee.

The Valley of Oblivion is the recognition of the futility of these manners of persuasions, for the real coherence of universal culture must stem from a practical determination of realistic values, the achievement of balance between the different categories of cultural contrasts and the deliberate cultivation of the factor and element of cultural moderation whereby harmony will be made to exist between incarnation, reincarnation and reinvention of cultural images, on the one hand, and the autonomy, affirmation, over-determination and disempowerment of cultural values, on the other.

Here then, begins the process of cultural purgation, not so much the cessation or attenuation of the search for immortality or the blissful state, but the acknowledgement that ideologies and geopolitical boundaries play little part in the sustenance of human cultural freedom. One need not have to dwell on the mountain top to thunder down oracular visions and timeless declarations for the inhabitants of a cultural valley (Nietzsche) to recognize that man plays a vital role in universal cultural security; that is, a liberated man who may owe no loyalty to statehood, religion and other restrictive cultural identities. This is to say that the earth cannot be an all-encompassing Elysium in that the transcendental injunctions of that realm dispense with the imperatives of determination, affirmation and reinvention.

In it, loyalty is absolute, and so is bliss, but being transcendental, it shrugs off the materiality of a visible cultural milieu and, to that extent, can only be understood within the imaginative terms set by material culture which has already surrendered its sovereignty in favour of a coherent cultural universe. The earth is for now the Infernal Regions of damnation, propelled, as it is, by the sanctimonious effusions of intolerable men in power whose very idea of human progress is essentially technocratic and not reconstructive in nature (Paepke's notion of the end of economic progress and the beginning of human transformation). Such a drive either towards economic and scientific attainments has arrested the free flow of cultural force (advanced polities) or have thwarted the beginning of the most basic social engineering processes (the so-called developing polities).

If anything, the earth must be made to accept certain cultural particulars of the Valley of Oblivion, and to illuminate this, we have a need to demonstrate what that valley looks like:

The Valley of Oblivion

> Aeneas perceived before him a spacious valley, with trees gently waving to the wind, a tranquil landscape, through which the river Lethe flowed. Along the banks of the stream wandered a countless multitude, numerous as insects in the summer air. Aeneas, with surprise, inquired who these were. Anchises answered, "they are souls to which bodies are to be given in due time. Meanwhile they dwell on Lethe's bank and drink, oblivious of their former lives ..." The creator, (Anchises told Aeneas), originally made the material of which souls are composed, of the

four elements, fire, air, earth and water, all which when united took the form of the most excellent part, fire, and became flame. This material was scattered like seed among the heavenly bodies, the sun, moon, and stars. Of this seed the inferior gods created man and all other animals, mingling it with various proportions of earth, by which its purity was alloyed and reduced. Thus the more earth predominates, in the composition, the less pure is the individual; and we see that men and women with their full-grown bodies have not the purity of childhood. So in proportion to the time which the union of body and soul has lasted, is the impurity contracted by the spiritual part. This impurity must be purged away after death, which is done by ventilating the souls in the current of winds, or merging them in water, or burning out their impurities by fire. Some few are admitted at once to Elysium, there to remain. But the rest, after the impurities of earth are purged away, are sent back to life endowed with new bodies, having had the remembrance of their former lives effectually washed away by the waters of the Lethe. Some souls, however, there still are, so thoroughly corrupted, that they are not fit to be entrusted with human bodies, and these pass by metempsychosis into the bodies of brute animals.
(*Classic Myths in English Literature*. PP. 351-352.)

There is little doubt that most mystic sequences derive their cognitive imperatives from the mythic rendition of cultural transcendence, the systematization of which is to be found in the Valley of Oblivion. The elements of incarnation, re-incarnation, and absolution of omissions, transcendental consciousness and affinity with the Godhead all lay their valid claims on the organic stature of this valley of re-evaluation. The problem with mysticism though, is that it accepts the transference of culture from its non-material, transcendental realm as a literal movement, and in not recognizing that the incarnation and re-classification of all the realms of cultural transcendence is a consequence of material knowledge. The strength of mysticism is its recognition that the movement out of the Valley of Oblivion, after the process of purification, to either Elysium or the Upper Air, is an individual burden and fate; it can never be a mass, collective exercise. So also is the degeneration into other lower planes of life (for example, the state of beast) as a consequence of deeply ingrained spiritual-cultural contamination which no rite of absolution can cleanse in a single purgatory process.

The greatest danger posed to human progress today is the search for collective amelioration via established states and polities. The search for Elysium must begin at the individual level and must be completed at the individual level. This is also true with regard to the quest for immortality and the State of Bliss. The Valley of Oblivion has a collection of multitudes, yet each member of the collective must answer specific individual questions. For mankind the same image must be sanctified; that is, that the search for cultural freedom and through that a state of social harmony must begin with specific individuals whose spiritual capacity endows them with the expansive, peculiar vision to utter words that may become valid generations after.

This process of achieving Elysium imposes minimal damage to cultural coherence, and will help in stifling those over assertive and disempowering mass illusions about the collective nature of a State of Bliss. The more the progress of culture is left in the hands of governments and universal institutions with their exaggerated assumptions about the potency of a determinate and defined world community, the more impotent is rendered the autonomy and capacity of values to be propelled by distinct human agents. The necessity of individuation as an unqualified imperative for the advancement of human and cultural conduct is a necessity recognized by mythic imagination, and a necessity that will lie at the base of human transformation.

One of the greatest harm inflicted on cultural progress in the current age is the non-recognition of different levels of cultural consciousness by leaders of different publics and the structures they create around mass institutions. Politicians and religious leaders are not the only culprits in insisting on an intolerable levelling down procedure whereby the attainment of a state of mass Elysium will become instantly possible. Part of the problem stems from the quantum academicization of social discourses in the university system the world over which has not only stultified intellectual creativity and imaginative thought but has also implanted in the system a worship or reverence of information over cultural and other facts.

When information becomes readily available; and in the absence of fact, all manners of people become pretenders to the possession of the basic ingredients of factual knowledge on which must subsist a successful encounter with and conquest of the Elysian Fields. From "scholarship", this levelling down process permeates research institutes and invention laboratories that, in turn, churn out mass bits of information particulars that are easily accessible but which inexorably demeans knowledge and stifles intellect. The World Wide Web is a ready example of this demeaning cultural process and is an issue I alluded to elsewhere.

However, the difference between mass seduction to the glory of Elysium with regard to religion, political governance and technological discoveries and inventions is quite clear. While religious symbolisms and rites of atonement and absolution are elements of a transcendental yearning for immortality and the securing for oneself and the collective a state of Elysium in the world hereafter, with allowance made for individual judgment at the realm of the Valley of Oblivion, masters of other social publics spawn and promote cultural artefacts, whose mass seductions are claimed to be empirically demonstrable within a determinate historical time.

A lesser degree of this danger is seen in the "peeling" off the years in which new technological products reach the mass level. As a Newsweek data shows:

Electricity (48 yrs); telephone (35 yrs); Gas automobile (55 yrs); radio (22 yrs); television (26yrs); microwave oven (30 yrs); personal computer, (16 yrs); mobile phone (13yrs); and the web, (7yrs). Thus, while it took the mass of the people 46 years (from 1873 – 1919) and 55 years, from (1886 – 1941) to enjoy the state of techno-cultural Elysium with regard to electricity and gas automobile respectively, it took them 7 years from (1991 – 1998) to enjoy the benefit of a new kind of a state of Elysian bliss: the web.

I consider this a lesser degree of cultural aberration in that the benefits of technology; that is, technology minus the complex consciousness, social complexities and cultural tensions it generates, must aid life, empower practical activities and elevate living standards. The only difference in this context is the web, wherein is reposed the tensions and contradictions of a techno-cultural age in that while it remains a technological invention, it radiates, through its expansive reach and inter-connectedness with other non-material aspects of cultural life, a multiplicity of cultural impetuses that delude its users that a new state of bliss has been attained or achieved.

A movement further away from the region of techno-cultural products and towards the centres of non-techno-cultural affirmations reveal a frightening dichotomy between the psychology of mass cultural intimations and the cultural realities of the postmodern age: freedom for all, equal right, brotherhood, fraternity, free world values, great democratic traditions and institutions accessible to all, individual liberty, etc, all which are peddled as reliable cultural products in today's cultural epoch.

The vulgarization of culture has led to licentiousness, mass illusion, mass hysteria and, ultimately, mass delusion about what the state, any state, is capable of affirming. And because an unbridgeable distance is necessarily created between the beacon of the Elysian Fields and the reality of the Infernal Regions, strategies and mechanisms are constantly deployed with the claim that they are temporary regressive cultural measures that will still make the attainment of a state of Elysium a successful one. This is essentially why the world has become and remains a police state, both at the level of the UN, and the various nation-states, developing and advanced, though the latter conceal these culturally regressive modes of control by an over-liberalized, licentious coating.

The bottom line remains that cultural self-realization is an end product of dynamic cultural processes; meaning that the attainment of any valid cultural ideal must be inherent in the pursuit of individual human entities who can interpret and assimilate their apprehension of the Elysian Fields and the significance of eternal bliss without the over determining will and disemboweling arrogance of a pseudo-universal cultural monolith.

Now, I make an acknowledgement. The quest for the Elysian Fields or the Islands of the Blessed is an eternal cultural one. This much must be admitted. Behind this quest lies the trembling nuance of immortality and state of bliss, both as a material cultural fact and a transcendental cultural yearning. Between these two axes lies the centre of cultural unconscious: the Valley of Oblivion, which provides the basis of inter-cultural overlaps and crossovers. This much must be again acknowledged. Because this quest is founded on the earliest human imagination which the classical mind incarnated and rendered as myth, it must continue as a response to man's desire to master nature through the complex social interrelationships he generated over the centuries that have become today's nation-states and polities.

The real cultural problem of today remains the over-simplification of a materially determined but transcendentally anchored mythic consciousness in such a way that the real assumptions of culture-in-transcendence are carried over into the realm of material culture. Myth cannot be demythologized in that its cultural terms are clear enough; the process of de-mythicization of culture must begin with the recognition that man, for now, is incapable of creating a state of Elysium here on earth, and neither can he achieve, in one fell swoop, that perfect world of eternal bliss or blessedness.

What he can hope to realize, using the limit situations of his social institutions, is to effect a crossover from the Infernal Regions of damnation which the universe is today to the transitional realm of the Valley of Oblivion which such institutions can accommodate. To attempt to do more than this is to inflict yet more damage on humanity's cultural health, particularly if such an attempt has to do with the realization of a collective state of immortality.

At a different level of cultural apprehension, the Elysian Fields, which is constantly energized by a blissful state of consciousness and being, recognizes only the validity of individual claims and individual determinations. To attain that plane of existence may, and always, will have nothing to do with the state of mass cultural persuasions or the type of polities and geographical boundaries that separate humanity from and against itself. It is a state of personal declaration, in that it achieves a leap over or equidistance from the unbalanced valley of indetermination and reinvention to the illumination, consciousness and freedom of the mountain top.

Chapter 7

BABI YAR: A METAPHOR OF HUMANITY

Images derived from:

Holocaust: The story of Man's Inhumanity to man: Part II: The Road to Babi Yar.

Setting: Babi Yar, a rural town in Ukraine.

Scenery: An Idyllic, almost Edenic grove pervaded by an Elysian aura minus the presence of the Jewish cemetery.

Context: One of the first gestures towards the effectuation of the Final Solution to the Jewish Question.

Dialogues: Random sampling:

Dorf: What is that over there? (paraphrase)

Major: The Jewish cemetery of Kiev, appropriate, isn't it?

Dorf: It means they don't deserve to live (then the mass slaughter began).

Helena: Women, the children ... Rudi, hold me.

Rudi: No one will believe any of this. They will say we lied. There is nobody who could do this to other people. (Later.)

Major: We will communicate with Headquarters later; give them the final tally.

Road Engineer: Tally?

Dorf: Yes (hesitating and self conscious), yes, bureaucratic stuff. (The denial continues throughout the jeep ride.)

Dorf: I can't wait to see my family. Without them, without Martha and the children, I don't know whether I can go on.

Final Tally: 33, 000 killed in two days.

I don't have access to the script of **Holocaust** I don't even own a slow playing VCR. Thus, the dialogue above, while not distorting the essential message in the text, is but an adumbration, a paraphrase. The first time I watched **Holocaust** was with a sense of horror. The second induced shock. The third was an embarrassing experience. However, after over 10 times of repeated viewing I came to the conclusion that the tragedy and triumph of the Weiss family desiderates the real texture of the human spirit, and that after all, Babi Yar is but a metaphor of humanity. Though not a historian, I have read my own fair share of the Second World War literature, particularly the volumes on the Jewish Holocaust, yet I remain unfulfilled, preferring instead to draw my imperatives from the spontaneous immediacy of a docu-drama such as **Holocaust**.

At long last, Western intellectuals have come to the inescapable conclusion that Hitlerism was not an historical aberration, but rather an organic end-product of the historical forces and processes that shape Western civilization. For John Lukacs[3] even, the essential revolutionary figure of the 20th century was neither Lenin nor Mao, but Hitler and its decisive ideological engine was nationalism and not communism or capitalist liberal democracy.

Going by the events in the then Soviet Union, Bosnia, and to an extent Somalia, and given the rapidly spreading centrifugal tendencies and tragedies in many nation-states the world over, particularly in Africa, along ethnic nationalities line, few can dispute Lukacs', claim. Beyond refutation, too, is the consequent cultural implication of this defining and re-inventive historical impulse: the fact that the Holocaust was not an historical and cultural aberration, but the objectification of man's concept of Elysium.

Hitler sought to extinguish the flame of Jewry in order to create a perfect state of blessedness for his chosen race and he did so, not as an isolated, alienated or individualized impetus, but in response to the propulsive yearnings of his generation. The same goes for Pol Pot who turned Kampuchea into a killing field and in just 4 years wiped out 3 million of his "contaminated" and "uneducable" people unprepared for the Elysium of his dream and vision. While it took Hitler about 6 years to systematically liquidate over 6 million Jews, and Pol Pot 4 years to cleanse his homeland of all undesirable elements, the Rwandan Hutus needed just a couple of months to fumigate close to a million Tutsis and moderate Hutus out of their blessed soil.

From Trujillo to Papa and Baby Doc; from Samoza to Marcos; from Ceausescu to Enver; from Idi Amin to Mobutu

---

[3] See *The End of the 20th Century* and the *End of the Modern Age*

Sese Seko; and from Samuel Doe to Marcias Nguema, humanity is defined by one metaphor: Babi Yar. Advanced societies are not spared his scourge, going by the events in Vietnam, and Afghanistan under Soviet indirect rule, the weapons of mass destruction deliberately acquired to annihilate humanity if the need arises, and the tens of thousands that are annually cut down in organized and individual violence and crimes. In all these historical and cultural instances, there is always to be encountered an imaginative leap from the known to the unknown: the exercise of will in aid of all manners of affirmations, and through that to create an Edenic universe of peace, contentment and moral perfection.

Deliberate acts of terror organized and unleashed by a state are directed towards a clear impulse: the need to preserve the sanctity of a determinate polity; the need to perpetuate the over-determining force in that polity; and the need to disempower all other contending social and cultural forces that impede the quest for Elysium. The process of this determination involves certain demarcated purgatory sequences, depending on the character of the perceived impediments and the instruments available for effectuating their reduction or elimination.

A common goal sustains this drive; a systematic rite of purification of incarnated elements, as in the Valley of Oblivion. Its consequence is also predictable; a cultural image of a new kind of Elysium that ultimately turns the earth into the Infernal Regions of damnation unrecognized by the impacting cultural forces, which remain inflexible in their vision of a new blissful state. The events at Babi Yar predated the enunciation of an irreversible Final Solution policy which Zyklon B. instrumented. This being the case, Dorf's squeamishness could be readily understandable in his sheer denial of the happenstances at the Edenic grove of Babi Yar. Subsequently, he is to become a machine-like, thoroughly distantiated enforcer of the concept of New Elysium.

Thereafter, at the war's end, three distinct cultural and socio-psychological images with a predictable underlying design became apparent among the remnants of the Nazi crowd: a deliberate denial or downgrading of the scale of the Holocaust as an arbitrary, unprogrammed side-consequence of a brutal war not because they were squeamish or revolted by what they did, but simply because their Elysium had collapsed, with all its implications for their individual survival; and a self-effacing, almost moronic declaration that they did what they did in obedience to orders from above; an order whose rejection or even less than enthusiastic execution will culminate in their own physical liquidation. The end result of this attitudinal disposition still remained a strategy in furtherance of the goal of post-war survival or personal preservation.

The third image was that of a studied or qualified repudiation of the scale of the Holocaust through recourse to individual and collective amnesia: I cannot recollect exactly what happened, who issued what particular directive or my personal role in executing such directive. Again, the organic impulse built around this amnesiac condition is the drive toward post-war self-perpetuation. Then was a universe, and most particularly a European theatre, rent by moral complex, cultural tension and an intricate patterning of conflicting historical processes, all of which combined to create, at the initial stages, a reluctant affirmation of the ideological, moral and racial perquisites of a State of Blessedness. It was the puritanical necessity of the Final Solution that liberated the conscience of the casual killers of Babi Yar into an unqualified acceptance of other weapons of destruction they dispensed with casual ease, and at enormous profit to these terror gangs.

The most exaggerated of this metaphor of humanity was the 1980 – 1988 Iraqi war of containment of Iranian Islamic fundamentalism with the active material and technical support of the industrial nations of the West, and the rest of the Gulf States who helped in financing and procuring the materials for her weapons programme. The first of the new Elysian testimony was against the Kurdish population with barely a murmur from the West. The second was at the Fao Marshes via chemical rain on thousands of Iranian troops with their silent approval.

The journey into Kuwait, actively aided and abetted by the West, was the highest transfiguration of the Iraqi State of Blessedness. Once in there, the West made sure that Saddam Hussein never got out. For the moment the Strait of Hormuz got threatened, the contest became one between affirmation and over-determination of will in the pursuit of an Elysian dream. The victory of the allied forces over Saddam's presidential guards lacks profound moral quality, in that its imperative necessity was the sustenance of an existing practical economic and commercial strategic agenda that was nearly toppled by a bellicose Iraqi assertiveness with the Elysium-incarnating weapons that the same West liberally endowed the state.

Saddam's only fatal error of judgement was his naive grasp of the fundamentals of a new humanity with interlocking geopolitical and strategic needs and dependencies, and his delusive pretentiousness about the pan-regional reach of his concept of new Elysium. Had he confined his affirmative strategies to his self-contained and geographically described sovereign boundaries, his promotion of his vision of Elysium, and through that, his affirmation of the cultural possibility of contemporary humanity would have gone largely unnoticed.

A cultural fact, not the truth of morality, is that nationalist excesses define the metaphor of humanity. And in the case of Bosnia-Herzegovina, its essential tragedy stems from the denial of this cultural fact (in combination with deep-rooted nationalist passion and ethos) in favour of an absurd sentimental moralizing. The moral of the Bosnian Civil War should not derive from the over-determination of ethical values over nationalist temper but rather from the recognition of each entity's search for a valid historical affirmation. The Elysium which the Othoman Turks incarnated at the apogee of their civilization had as its substratic element the ethnic cleansing of other national configurations which reached its high watermark in the 1492 massacre of virtually the whole adult Serbia population in Sarajevo.

Because very few people ever paused to consider what Moslems are doing today in the heart of Europe; how they got there; and the nationalist-cultural ethos they spawned over the centuries (an altogether a de-ethical issue in my mind), it will be difficult for them to appreciate the Serbian eagerness in unfurling their ethnic cleansing banner over the whole of Greater Yugoslavia. Such a repetitive pattern of historical metaphor was to be seen even in the events leading up to the First World War and thereafter, and again during the Second World War when the Croatian and Muslim populations of Yugoslavia aided the Hitlerites in the creation of their own very idea of new Elysium.

The Bosnian conflict lacked any worthwhile moral equation, and was devoid of any authentic ethical paradigm, on all the sides that were involved in it. The real historical-cultural forces at work is the resolution, at a qualitatively higher historical plane, of a long tradition of persuasions wherein is self-contained and self regulated the metaphor of humanity we have already described. Each contending entity was engaged in the search for sustainable historical and cultural links, and justified such a quest through the mutual annihilation of other opposing forces.

Ethnic cleansing, therefore, is another metaphor of humanity, not as an isolated experiment in Bosnia, but as an organic expression of all Elysian dreams: the Red Indian/Native Americans in the USA; the Blacks in Apartheid South Africa; the Aborigines in Australia; and the dislocation and relocation of the Scots from their homeland to Northern Ireland. That Bosnian "war criminals" and all others who committed "crimes against humanity" are being tried today in The Hague should not be read as a moral issue, but rather as the relative incapacity of such sponsors of humanity's metaphor to successfully effectuate their concept of Elysium. They are being tried by a more formidable, over-determining force (an amorphous international community) whose triumphal presence is an indication of a specifically patterned globalized new Elysium.

Very few people will deny the fact that had the USSR not collapsed and Euro-communism forced on retreat, the outcome of the Bosnian Civil War would have been the elevation, to a new state of glory, of Serbian heroism and complementary revolutionary staunchness. Not a single American, British, French or German soldier would have dared set his foot on Bosnian soil or in any other place in Greater Yugoslavia. If the Bosnian-Serbs are being tried (many are still being hunted for trial) for shared moral concerns over their nationalist excesses, and not on the basis of the ineffectuality of their Elysian dream, why are the founding fathers (and their descendants), of America, Australia, virtually the whole of Europe and the white South Africans not also being arraigned at The Hague for their ethnic cleansing drives against native Americans, the Australian Aborigines, millions of Blacks who passed through the Door of No Return at Goree during the slave trade, and the massive dislocation and extermination of black populations during the apartheid era, respectively?

They are not being tried because of their successful affirmation of the metaphor of humanity which Babi Yar is; and because through that they ensured the triumphal presence of their various concepts of the State of Blessedness. Because the South African historical and cultural contradictions were resolved via negotiation, what they had in the place of a Human Rights Tribunal was a Truth and Reconciliation Commission as a means of confronting the nation's collective pains, memories and remembrances, and the purgation of past historical oddities.

Other contemporary indications of this metaphor of humanity are to be seen in the Somali, Rwandan and Burundi experiences in the past few years. Somalia became a failed state, as many other states are bound to fail, as a consequence of the inability of the contending clans to work out a realistic framework in their pursuit of Elysium. The tragic fallouts of this irresolution include a savage civil war, millions of dead, dying, malnourished and displaced persons and an economy and a cultural fabric that has already collapsed. As for Rwanda, very few people are bothered about the Tutsi possession of power, authority and influence in spite of their demographic status and, through that, the successful effectuation of their idea of Elysium.

The Hutu historical and cultural challenge which created a human mess of nearly a million body counts, for all its excesses, was a reactive and not a proactive phenomenon. The containment of that challenge has now become the substance of universal moral reproach and not the morality of the challenge itself. Had they succeeded in creating their own Elysium they would have successfully concealed those ethnic excesses and made the ethical issue a dubious world agenda. Check, in this regard, the late Kabila-led forces in the Democratic Republic of the Congo whose triumphal historical presence and effectuated Elysian state more than concealed their nationalist excesses during their process of historical affirmation, or more recently, the mass murder committed by NATO forces in Libya in their successful attempt of deconstructing the late Col Gaddaffi's Elysian Fields.

What holds true for Rwanda is equally valid with regard to Burundi, and may be before long, Nigeria, where an over-determining state structure, which having mastered the polity, may cause a national implosion through its excessive quest for a new kind of national Elysium.[4]

Babi Yar is a symbol of cultural crossover. Apart from the fact that the transposition of a transcendental cultural

---

[4] This part of the essay was written in early 1998 during the dictatorship of the late Gen. Sani Abacha in Nigeria.

paradigm (Elysian Fields; Elysium; State of Blessedness; State of Bliss; etc) into the realm of material culture not only creates historical and cultural tensions, but leads to an inexorable descent from the Valley of Oblivion to the Infernal Regions of Hades, a greater measure of this crossover is to be seen in the arrested animation of determination and affirmation by an over-determining historical-cultural impetus intent on achieving its end at all cost. The higher the degree of this crossover, the deeper the scale of the incarnated cultural metaphor, and the more profound and sustained its elasticity, constancy, regularity and repetitiveness.

It is on the basis of this historical and cultural fact that Babi Yar ceases to be an aberrant and revolting cultural image, but a self-contained thesis about the contemporary state and status of humanity. Yet, before we examine other shaping cultural forces at work in the validation of this metaphor, another historical and cultural fact must be established: the realization that a new Jewish Elysium cannot be guaranteed outside the Jewish homeland; and a resolve that the knitting of a co-ordinate Jewish cultural mosaic can only occur in a defined geographical polity led to the founding of the State of Israel on the premise of never again shall it happen to Jews anywhere in the world.

Here now is what history and mankind's cultural evolution teaches; that is, that man has not always been an Elysian visionary at the earliest stage of material incarnation, and neither has the metaphor of Babi Yar been a consciously yearned for human possibility. One can begin to appreciate the emergence of this metaphor by searching for historical parallels to Anthony Burgess' thinly fictionalized *The Kingdom of the Wicked*. For at his original state of material incarnation, man was merely baffled by the immensity of the natural environment and all the phenomena located therein; baffled and embarrassed by his initial incapacity to effectuate any meaningful material and other presences on earth.

Thus, bafflement and embarrassment were the driving forces in man's earliest encounter with nature; and through that he started to produce and reproduce a culture of self-preservation. The murders he committed, against other earthly beasts, and against other men, including the element of cannibalism, were solely directed at the most minimal level of autonomy of value; instinct for survival, self-preservation, and ultimately self-perpetuation. The metaphor of Babi Yar which derives from the vision of a New Elysium is a product of a culture of contentment, and only occurred at the historical stage of community-building, interlocking of social relationships, and the pursuit of power, authority and glory; values which by their very inherent determination could only be effectuated by the complete contamination of autonomously existing values.

It is the fact of sociology, ethnology and cultural studies that as human communities become more organized, regulated and systematized with binding social contracts and structures of power, authority, obedience and group response, so did the transfiguration of human needs from their basic material premises into non-material, cultural categories. It is not that the spiritualization of culture was not a fact of man's earliest material presence on earth; rather at that stage of cultural evolution man's spiritual consciousness and transcendental imagination was only created to aid his basic self-preservative quest. At the later stage of human transcendental, non-material affirmations this urge became merely the pursuit of pleasure. It is out of this pursuit of pleasure and the search for contentment that the vision of a new Elysium emerged, and with that the signification of humanity's metaphor.

We readily see this with regard to the pyramid-building Pharaohs of Egypt; the classical despots of China; the adventures of Alexander the Great; the imperial expansionist paradigms of Caesar, Genghis Khan and Kublai Khan; the Napoleonic vision of a New Earth; and Shaka's creative use of the *assegai* to enact a new Zulu Elysium. Again, from the

Crusaders to the Ottoman Turks; and from the Holy Roman Empire's Spanish Inquisition to the nationalist ferments in Europe during the 16th, 17th, 18th and 19th centuries, cultural-historical over-determining impetuses subsisted on this imaginative reconstruction of a transcendental Elysian Fields on earth, and to achieve that, the energizing of the weapons of mass murder as a sanctifying metaphor.

Therein, too, is located the Western world's imperial quest for colonies, the contradictions of which led in part to the First World War (the break-up of the decaying Ottoman and Austro-Hungarian empires and the emergence of new globalized Elysian Fields: Britain, the USA, and to a lesser degree, France). For Russia, the war was a propulsive force that shattered the Czarist autocracy and the erection, in its place, of a New Communist Elysium. The rest, as we know, beginning with Stalin, Mussolini, Franco and Hitler, and continuing right up to Pol Pot's Kampuchea, Bosnia, Rwanda, Burundi, Somalia and, predictably, into the foreseeable future, in several national directions, are elemental testaments of the central, mainstream tradition in mankind's historical and cultural evolution.

What, then, are the regulating, increasingly systematized properties of this metaphor? In a simple, schematic rendition, the constitutive shaping forces are self-contained within the following matrices; an organic connectedness that has an inherent etiological logic:

i. The metaphor of Babi Yar is a cultural revolt against the original thesis of affirmation.
ii. Through such a successful revolt the attenuation of the autonomy of values takes effect.
iii. Such a metaphor occurs at the level of over-determination of values.
iv. Yet, to effectuate all manners of over-determination, the process of disempowerment of values is achieved.
v. Such a universal cultural thesis is authenticated via a process of transposition of values from one cultural

realm to another; in specific terms, through the subordination of material culture to cultural transcendence, which is, then, realized in images, concepts, mental constructs and beliefs as material culture.

vi. The materialization of cultural transcendence occurs with the specific image of an envisioned Elysium in mind.

vii. Such an image is the product of a "culture of contentment" whereby the individually incarnated, autonomously existing paradigms of basic material self-preservation are transfigured, at a higher level of organized community, into the search for collective perfection.

viii. It is at this stage that cultural subordination becomes the metaphor of humanity.

ix. Going by verifiable historical and cultural indications, the sustenance of this metaphor, together with its Elysian prospects, is ensured via certain structures of ideological loyalties, chief among which are ethnic nationalism and political philosophy/ideology.

x. The systematic nature of this metaphoric paradigm, its universal-globalized reach, and its regularity and repetitiveness are all indications that its organic impulse subsists within the mainstream tradition of mankind's historical and cultural evolution.

xi. Nevertheless, in the realization of this historical and cultural vision, enormous distortions occur in that the attempt to prefigure a transcendental cultural desire into the realm of material culture produces a journey which creates neither the desired Elysian state nor even the Valley of Oblivion, but the transformation of humanity into Infernal Regions of waste.

xii. The ethical issues involved in this metaphor pertain more to this question of violation of established Natural Laws and less on the material scale of the Infernal Regions, as profound as this may be.

xiii. This is so in that such ethical issues are ethical to the extent that such Elysian dreamers or visionaries fail to effect their successful historical and cultural presence, for were they to achieve this triumphal presence a new set of ethical considerations, different and opposed to that occasioned by a failed cultural and historical realization, becomes the only valid or authentic ethics. (Check, for example, what the ethics of the Nazi Holocaust would have been had Hitler triumphed over the Allied Forces or had Pol Pot still remained in power till date, or had the Hutu "extremists" seized and retained power successfully till date.

Contrast this ethical picture with the triumphal presence of European settlers over the Native American cultural milieu, the successful presence of Australian settler community over the Australian aboriginal population, or the ethical reality in South Africa, notwithstanding a pretentious global approbation over racial oppression, had apartheid endured till date).

The interconnectedness of these theses substantially explains the perceptual or cognitive difficulty in appreciating their full substance. Previous intellectual and philosophical-political traditions have always sought to localize such a metaphoric image within determinate, self-contained geo-polities. They are desiderated as incidental historical and cultural aberrations, which are located outside mankind's mainstream historical and cultural evolution. Attempts were even made, including efforts by some exponents of the Frankfurt School of Critical Theory and Cultural Studies, to subject the principal architects of this metaphor to the most rigorous psychiatric and psychoanalytic evaluations (from a distance, of course, and essentially based on their pronouncements, writings, and observable behaviour), with the ready conclusion that they were or are merely socio-and psychopathic mass murderers with deviant, demonic capacities.

Such intellectual illusions were even sustained right to

the regime of Pol Pot and other lesser seekers of various forms of new Elysium in this generation. It took the disintegration of the Soviet Union along ethnic nationalities line, the Bosnian Civil War, and the Somali, Rwanda and Burundi situations for the desirable re-orientation of intellectual consciousness to occur at the level of historical cognition and cultural perception of the real, fundamental forces that have been shaping human evolution. As complex as this metaphor is, and as contradictory as its practical effectuation may be, the essential substance of a bold and liberated intellectual tradition (devoted to its study) is the honest admission that we have all along been dealing with a fundamental, inescapable cultural and historical fact of all ages, past and present.

Here again is another cultural fact. The non-mass effectuation of this metaphor does not constitute a disruption of this organic cultural and historical process. This is to say, that the search for a State of Blessedness need not demand or even accommodate any genocidal strategy. The selective elimination of political opponents by those who nurse this vision of an Elysium will more than compensate, depending on the determinate political, cultural and historical realities on the ground, for extra mass measures may not, in fact, be necessary.

Even though the body counts rose steeply during all of Pinochet's Elysian moments in Chile his own brand of Babi Yar was effected through the physical liquidation of Salvador Allende and a couple of other leaders of his government, in addition to the carefully planned and orchestrated disappearances of scores of political opponents and civil society leaders. This same is true with regard to the State of Blessedness in Suharto's Indonesia which was instrumented via the extermination of Sukarno and the top-ranking communist-nationalist cadres of his regime. Again, as in the case of Pinochet, the body count kept rising before Suharto was forced out of power in May 1998.

What, therefore, establishes Babi Yar as mankind's cultural metaphor is not the scale of its mass reach or the limited nature of its realization, but rather its organic design, structure and character. As stated earlier, the search for a new Elysium always involves a historical and cultural vision; what stands as fact is the quest itself. The strategy of effectuating this determinate vision will always depend on variegated historical and cultural impulses, and the specific nature of the social milieu which will either make for a near instinctual realization of deeply held cultural impetuses, wherein is located the compulsion towards mass exercise, or the subtle affirmation of the envisioned State of Blessedness, wherein is reposed the limited over-determination of sanctified values.

In this diverse contradictory cultural situation is located mankind's moral dilemma, for while the second course of action seemingly raises no ethical dust because of its situatedness within the ambit of collective-universal moral world order the first course of action is considered an apparent disruption of universal ethical standards and, to that extent, depending on the end-result of this realized vision (triumphal presence or arrested animation), it almost always generates moral approbation and spiritual denunciation.

Again, the lesson of Babi Yar is that mankind is always crossing cultural boundaries that aid the affirmation of values. Such cultural crossovers, from the material to the transcendental, and from the transcendental back to the material, leads not only to the distortion of the real meaning and purpose of existence but ends up inflicting enormous damage on nature itself. Here again, it must not be denied that the most elemental cultural incarnation of material value, at its most basic stage of production and evolution, is the search for historical validity among all human entities. The quest for validity must be recognized as the systematic apprehension of nature and all its phenomena and properties; the regulated desire for mastery of the material universe; and the conditioning of all cultural products that will aid man in his historical search for meaning.

Now, again, we perceive another cultural reality. The quest for authenticity must, of course, lead to the prioritization of the basic elements of self-preservation, self perpetuation and instinctual immortality. To achieve this, values must not only be incarnated but must be qualitatively and qualitatively transformed to aid this process. Such a mechanism of incarnation and transformation must, of necessity, impact negatively on the autonomous existence of values through affirmation, over-determination and disempowerment. Though all manners of cultural reinventions wreak havoc on the original human thesis of basic determination of want, they still express a high degree of cultural coherence and, to this extent, contain tolerable cultural visions. While a consonant cultural world order, as against a dissonant cultural consciousness and sensibility which is always harmful by its over-assertiveness and over-determination, is the ideal, desirable cultural state, a materially dissonant cultural attitude is always the reality that must be accepted and endured. Such an endurance and acceptance subsist on the parameter of the relativity of cultural affirmation and over-determination that helps in keeping the cultural milieu in a constant state of flux, dynamism and conflict.

This cultural image remains opposed to the search for the State of Blessedness or new Elysian Fields, for to accommodate this quest, man begins to shed his basic material instincts, and places in its place an absolutist cultural vision. Because of the cultural crossovers we have already alluded to, this absolutist vision of a new Elysium must thus harness a hidden metaphor of cultural disavowal that leads inexorably to the Babi Yar experience. At this state of the demonstration of cultural presence, the reality of individual and collective perpetuation becomes lost in the grand quest for a State of Bliss. Such a state, if it must incarnate its blissful paradigms, must demolish all existing cultural elements and forces that stand in its way, as a precondition for its triumphal presence.

The search for historical perfection, both at the ideal and

real states of cultural experience, must always cause a descent from the high expectations of Elysian affirmation to the lowest depths of mankind's Infernal Regions. When this occurs, depending, as we have already established, on the success or otherwise of such a historical sought for cultural vision, energy is spent in the pursuit of the incarnation of such a metaphor and not on the driving, propulsive motivations that made it occur in the first place.

What is, therefore, being stressed is a recurring pattern of a given cultural reality; the ethical question, like all moral enigmas, only mean something depending on the collective realization of the cultural and historical forces at work and the capacity of groups and entities to arrest the further incarnation of this animated historical and cultural presence. They are only ethical issues on the basis of their end-results (success or failure) and not on the basis that such metaphoric statements fall outside the mainstream tradition of mankind's historical and cultural evolution.

To handle such an ethical dilemma depends less on the appeal to the sentimental spirituality of a de-spiritualized age but to boldly accept that what has occurred is indeed irreversible and, in this context, to deploy strategies and mechanisms in future which will help in forestalling such occurrences. This, as we have alluded to, is part of the reason why the State of Israel is in existence today, and part of that state's sometimes impassioned and oftentimes fanatical devotion to the cause of its historical substance and perpetuation. The lesson of Israel is a lesson for all historical and cultural entities in the world, notwithstanding the fact that in the aggressive pursuit of its historical and cultural justification, Israel has succeeded in inflicting its own Elysian vision on the state and people of Palestine, who in turn must seek their own relevance through a just struggle for historical and cultural affirmation.

Chapter

MASTERS OF CONSCIOUSNESS

Beginning

Illumination is startling in its immediacy. Yet, this immediacy is a concession to ignorance. Those who are masters of consciousness; that is, those who embody reality in its totality are never seduced by epiphany for illumination is part of their being. This force derives but a little from intellectual habit; its mainstream flows from instinct nourished over time.

Such masters achieve their greatest strength when they celebrate values in their purest and, as it were, freest form. Beyond this admission is opened up to us a series of contentions about the place of value in man's cultural evolution and the capacity of such masters to either affirm, determine or disempower reality. Our agreement or disagreement with such perceptions will involve the most scrupulous scrutiny of their fidelity and concession to the originality, conventionality and, this is very important, the legitimacy of all value-systems and life-forms.

Karl Marx is the greatest social and political thinker of all times. The value he discovered – that of change as primarily a determination of economic impulses – lies till today at the root of most social processes. The formal purity of dialectical materialism subsists on its non-prescriptivist character; it only aims at explaining as objectively as possible those nuances of change whose legitimacy derives from conflict of interest. And because contradiction, at the planes of being and social consciousness, defines man's relationship with matter and other men, so will the culture and civilization of man remain an end-product of this conflicting relationship. Cultural processes may habour material facts as Raymond Williams tried to demonstrate in *Marxism and Literature, The Country and the City* and *The Long Revolution,* yet the main carrier of change, as Marx found, lies in man's historical capacity to transform his state of affirmation and the conditions of his state through a regulated and accidental process of conflict, accommodation and continuity located mainly on the material foundations of nature.

To this extent, therefore, the most profitable way of studying the qualitative and quantitative succession of new social, cultural and historical types, including the evolution of post-communist and post-Marxist societies, is through the most consistent application of the laws of dialectics as enunciated by Marx. His immortality as a formulator of a certain kind of value – that is, change conditioned by material life is his merciless exposition of the inner law of conflict which in our age has over-complicated some of his political and ideological assumptions. It is in this regard that his intellectual habit and instinctual conduct are to be seen more in *The German Ideology, A Contribution to the Antique of Political Economy* and *The Poverty of Philosophy* and less in *The Communist Manifesto* and *Das Capital.*

The simple explanation for this is that while the first range of works affirm the freedom of various value-types and accommodate the autonomy of life-forms even in their mutual exclusiveness, without the interjection of tendentious formulae, the latter named works not only over determine specific political and ideological values over others, but also disempower men's apprehensible capacities. Their essential complexity is that while the dialectics of change is infinitely capacious in its scientific investigation of all manners of materially determined social and cultural transformations, the ideology of communism, with its social engineering techniques and strategies, is time-bound in its problematic over-derivation of the final status of humanity.

• • • • • •

Nietzsche – the most intense and profound philosopher of the modern age – gave humanity back its common sense through a pitiless assault on the foundation of all manners of orthodoxy. His rejection of universal moral principle, moral criteria and moral world order was his first contribution to the study of cultural evolutionism. His piercing insight led him to the discovery that beneath all historically and culturally binding value systems and moral formulations, subsists the tyranny of a few individuals, particularly members of the political and theological classes to deform and asphyxiate reality after their own image.

What people believe in, according to Nietzsche, and the sum total of all collectively ascribed moral and ethical injunctions is nothing but the partially selective perception of reality by an insignificant percentage of humanity. Thus, the dominance and marginality of certain cultural traits, particularly the evolution and process of adding value to things, events and phenomena, has nothing whatsoever to do with their inherent natural authenticity. The legitimacy or otherwise – that is the valuableness of a thing – is nothing short of historical prejudice nursed over time and space.

However, the revaluation of values need not encourage any form of moral excesses, for properly defined and understood such a revaluation may even be the solution to mankind's moral crisis. The crisis of morality, in Nietzsche's calculation, does not stem from the multiplicity of contending ethical affirmations, all claiming legitimacy, but the ability of a few powerful members of the human community to impose their particular kind of value on the rest. Thus, permissiveness is not a moral category, being a reaction against anti-liberal statutes; permissiveness is, again, not a means towards the achievement of the autonomy of values in so far as the values so permitted by society and individuals do not relate to a pure, inner feeling. They only allude to certain manners of intuition that is opposed to mastered instinct; that is to say, they only explain a response that has already been over-determined by the very structure of value in a given human order. For when values are revaluated and are made free and autonomous, within the larger dimension of a state desirous of achieving collective cultural possibility of meaningfulness, each and every individual, while still retaining original differential essences, will relate to and accommodate one another with less probability of cultural tension even when those differentials are made cogent.

Apart from the revaluation of values, Nietzsche's strength as a philosopher draws from his studied disinterest in banal or mundane activities, of which, whether we like it or not, politics constitutes the highest exaltation. One of the remarkable dilemmas of the 20th century is precisely that the philosopher who most opposed the utter ordinariness of politics and politicians; who scorned statecraft as an unworthy human venture; and who evolved the metaphor of mountain-top dwelling from which one can look down into the meaningless din and clatter in the valley below, was himself appropriated by several vulgar political movements as a way of rationalizing and reinforcing their half-baked political theories and contemptible pseudo-ideologies. Nietzsche was a philosopher's philosopher-intense, haughty, complicated and yet sublimely humane.

Not one to be seduced by spiritual transcendence, being an embodiment of illumination itself, he was however separated from every day reality in order to find the right depth and balance to manifest his oracular declarations. I quite insist with him that the mountain-top is the highest stage and place of mental exultation, a near sovereign region of consciousness from which one thunders down timeless exercise of truth "in which time but tries its teeth in vain". To achieve this plane of reality is to renounce all prejudices which culture harbours and to establish, in their proper significations, the authenticity of all values that approximate man's understanding of self and his universe.

Another element I find enchanting in Nietzsche is his ready admission that knowledge, of the most intense and poignant variety, is not the stuff that ought to be consumed anyhow, by just anybody. This intellectual attitude has nothing to do with arrogance; neither has it anything in common with the incomprehensibility of virtually all theological truths and ecclesiastical testimonies. It simply means that the philosophic vocation carries with it the burden of constant historical evidence and proof beyond its age and time. Such a proof is thus not dependent on the immediacy of cognition and apprehension; those two categories properly belong to a later historical time for full manifestation.

This being the case, the capacity of an average mind to apprehend the thoughts of the moment is only possible in situations whereby those thoughts have average mental and intellectual capacity. The full examination of a philosophic system, for example, a value-system such as we are interested in, will await the passage of several seasons, generations and even a millennium. This is precisely why philosophic truths which are spurned in their time are constantly being affirmed and even over-determined in another age with a different aura of awareness. This is to say that a great benefit awaits the few who can scrutinize the elemental truth of today; the future belongs to the rest of humanity who lack the capacity of finding meaning and logic in their age.

However, my quarrel with Nietzsche is his eventual over-determination of those values he adored, and the disempowerment of those others he held in absolute contempt. Such a transition from the revaluation of values to the reconstruction of values may have emanated out of the fear of the formlessness of existence which chaos, nihilism and cultural disorder – as a consequence of the legitimacy of all value-forms – will portend. This need not be so, for a greater moral crisis flows out of this over-determination of and reaction against certain images in nature, for the reconstruction of value leads inexorably to the erection of an ethical system with the possibility of 'it' being universalized as a moral standard of measure. Reconstruction in turn involves restoration, of which the will to power, among other wills, and the towering image of the superman, for example, are but inherent determinations. It is on this calculation that I base his purest, and by extension, greatest philosophic discoveries on *Beyond Good and Evil* and *Revaluation of all Values* and not, as many will assume, on *Thus Spoke Zarathustra, Twilight of the Idols* and *The Anti-Christ*.

The Voice of the Master on: Revaluation of Values

"The principal stages in the history of the sensations by virtue of which we make anyone accountable for his actions, that is to say, of the moral sensations, are as follows. First of all, one calls individual actions good or bad quite irrespective of their motives but solely on account of their useful or harmful consequences. Soon, however, one forgets the origin of these designations and believes that the quality 'good' and 'cost' is inherent in the actions themselves, irrespective of their consequences: thus committing the same error as that by which language designates the stone itself as hard, the tree itself as green - that is to say, by taking for cause that which is effect. Then one consigns the being good or being evil to the motives and regards the deeds in themselves as morally ambiguous. One goes further and accords the predicate good or evil no longer to the individual motive but to the whole nature of a man out of whom the motive grows as a plant does from the soil. Thus one successively makes men accountable for the effects they produce, then for their actions, then for their motives, and finally for their nature.

"Now one finally discovers that this nature, too, cannot be accountable, in as much as it is altogether a necessary consequence and assembled from the elements and influences of things past and present; that is to say, that man can be made accountable for nothing; not for his nature, nor for his motives, nor for his actions, nor for the effects he produces. One has thereby attained to the knowledge that the history of the moral sensations is the history of an error, the error of accountability which rests on the error of freedom of will. No one is accountable for his deeds; no one for his nature; to judge is the same thing as to be unjust. This applies when the individual judges himself. The proposition is as clear as daylight and yet here everyone prefers to retreat back into the shadows and untruth: from fear of the consequences.

"The concept good and evil has a two-fold pre-history: firstly in the soul of the ruling tribes and castes. He who has the power to requite good with good, evil with evil, and also actually practices requital – that is to say, grateful and revengeful – is called good; he who is powerless and cannot requite accounts as bad. As a good man one belongs to the 'good', a community which has a sense of belonging together because all the individuals in it are combined with one another through the capacity for requital. As a bad man one belongs to the 'bad', to a swarm of subject powerless people who have no sense of belonging together. The good are a caste, the bad a mars like grams of sand. Good and bad is for a long time the same thing as noble and base, master and slave."

Human, All too Human, p. 39

On Dwelling on the Mountain-top

"The conditions under which one understands me and then necessarily understands – I know them all too well. One must be honest in intellectual matters to the point of harshness to so much as endure my seriousness, my passion. One must be accustomed to living on mountains – to seeing the wretched ephemeral chatter of politics and national egoism beneath one. One must have become indifferent, one must never ask whether truth is useful or whether it is a fatality ... A preference, born of strength, for questions for which no one today has the courage; courage for the forbidden; pre-destination for the labyrinth. An experience out of seven solitudes: new ears for new music. New eyes for the most distant things; a new conscience for truths which have hitherto remained dumb, and the will to economize in grand style; to keeping one's force, one's enthusiasm in bounds. Reverence for oneself; love for oneself; unconditional freedom with respect to oneself ...

"Very well! These alone are my readers, my rightful readers, my predestined readers: what do the rest matter? – The rest are merely mankind – one must be superior to mankind in force, in loftiness of soul – in contempt..."

The Anti-Christ, Foreword

On The Art of Incomprehension

"One does not want only to be understood when one writes but just as surely not to be understood. It is absolutely no objection to a book if anyone finds it unintelligible: perhaps that was part of its author's intention – he did not want to be understood by "anyone". When it wants to communicate itself, every nobler spirit and taste also selects its audience; in selecting them it also debars 'the others'. All the more subtle rules of style have their origin here: they hold at arm's length, they create distance, they forbid 'admission', understanding – while at the same time they alert the ears

of those who are related to us through their ears."
Gay Science, p. 381

"If this writing is unintelligible to anyone and jars on his ears the fault is, it seems to me, not necessarily mine. It is clear enough, assuming, as I do, that one has read my earlier writings and has not spared some effort in doing so; for they are not easily accessible."
On the Genealogy of Morals, Preface, p. 8

"But who knows, after all, whether I even wish to be read today? – To create things upon which time tries its teeth in vain; in form and in substance to strive for a little immortality – I have never been modest enough to demand less of myself."
Expeditions of an Untimely Man, p. 51

"I am one thing, my writings are another – Here, before I speak or touch on the question of their being understood or not being understood. I shall do so as perfunctorily as is fitting. For the time for this question has certainly not yet come. My time has not yet come, some are born posthumously – one day or other institutions will be needed in which people live and teach as I understand living and teaching: perhaps even chairs for the interpretations of Zarathustra will then be established. But it would be a complete contradiction of myself if I expected ears and hands for my truths already today: that I am not heard today, that no one today knows how to take from me, is not only comprehensible, it even seems to me right.

"Ultimately, no one can extract from things, book included, more than he already knows. What one has no access to through experience, one has no ear for.

"Whoever believed he had understood something of me had dressed up something out of me after his own image. Whoever had understood nothing of me denied that I came into consideration at all."
Ecce Homo: Why I Write Such Excellent Books, p. 1

• • • • • •

Many today forget that when Albert Einstein wrote that "Great Spirits have always found violent opposition from mediocrities" and "that the latter cannot understand it when a man does not thoughtlessly submit to hereditary prejudices but honestly and courageously uses his intelligence," he wrote with regard to Bertrand Russell who spent a lifetime waging a ceaseless battle against superstition and ignorance, exploding myths and de-constructing legends – in morals and manners, metaphysics and religion. As a master of enlightenment, he extended the boundaries of science and mathematics, logic and clear thought, interrogating an authoritarian universal value system with passion and uncommon commitment, always alert to its shaping sources of origin and nuances, and forever rendering authentic the self-imbedded autonomy of all life-forms.

For Russell, the unity of the human enterprise does not lie in the canonization of mythic structures aspiring to universal moral, spiritual, and social claim, and reinforced by the exaggerated powers of implacable political and theocratic institutions and authorities. For him, victory over existential despair, angst and ennui is a consequence of humanity's eternal yearning for release from mental prison; a perpetual search for affirmation that is opposed to immanent orthodoxies and ossified conventionality.

For him, also, to doubt is to begin the journey of self-discovery; to reject notions which appear settled; to liberate human thought, passion, belief and conduct in various directions; and to unfurl the banner of agnostic faith and skepticism in the cognition and interpretation of reality, all reality, value, all value.

• • • • • •

Lenin was the greatest political figure of the 20th century and, after Marx, the greatest political philosopher of the modern age. Just as Marx discovered the element of change and continuity through conflict and unity of opposites in national parameters, Lenin's extension of the dialectics of change encompassed the universe as an integral entity. Because Marx never fully anticipated the international character of capital, it was left to Lenin to seek out the ways the resolution of the conflict of value could occur at the global level. His strength does not lie in his ability to mobilize the Bolsheviks against the reactionary Czarist autocracy (a case of two distinctly existing autonomous values struggling for legitimacy); rather, it lay in his objective assessment of the inter-relationship between universal entities and his discovery that the strength of one (capitalism) lies in its internationalization of contradictions (imperialism), while its weakness stems from the assertion of the autonomy of the values directly impacted upon by such a force (national liberation struggles of the colonial dependencies).

When he stressed that imperialism's weakest link remained its colonial possessions, he only projected a fact beyond the range of politics and ideology for the real content of that assertion is that in all human undertakings, in all natural phenomena, and in all real situations, particularly those whose achievement of value is dependent on a tenuous universal term of reference, the beginning of freedom is the assertion of the sovereign status of all values, and the restriction to its legitimate zones, of those other values whose universal claims are false. It is in this direction that one can fully appreciate his insights; that nothing in life should be taken for granted, and granted life as they appear; that no matter how dressed up a reality is, it can never have legitimate properties beyond its credible boundaries; and that the current debate over the multiplicity of centres of cultural affirmations must begin with a thorough understanding and appreciation of the relevance of each and every single social ingredient in life. This is, notwithstanding its cultural circumstances wherein could be ascribed to it the element of dominance and marginality at any phase or point in mankind's evolution.

* * * * * *

One of the greatest hoaxes of all ages, literary and non-literary, is the legend that William Shakespeare, the poet and dramatist, was an uncouth, ill-educated Stratford-upon-Avon deer thief who hounded his debtors to misery and despair and was barely able to scratch out his unlettered signature on a pre-designed epitaph. The tragedy of Shakespeare's story is not even the fact that Edward de Vere, the 17th Earl of Oxford, who authored those immortal works, was forced by compelling historical, social and cultural circumstances to shed his identity which the Stratford lay-about Will Shakespeare appropriated, but that this transmutation of identity carried with it a whole range of dangerous assumptions that are significant to our understanding of value.

Charlton Ogborn shouldn't have written a good work to prove this point for even a high school late-developer would immediately grasp the identity of the man behind the works through a perfunctory study of just one of his plays. The crisis of value which emerges out of the ascription of Shakespeare's identity to an unworthy contemporary is remarkably illustrated in Will Durant's comparison of the subject to Francis Bacon in his illuminating work, *The Story of Philosophy*. This is precisely because had Durant known or believed otherwise, he would have shown restraint in his apprehension of Shakespeare's motive forces, inner psychology and perception of value. For once Durant and virtually the whole intellectual world made their mistake, there emerged a near capricious misinterpretation and misrepresentation of the values and ideas inherent in Shakespeare's works to the extent that today any analytic exercise that goes beyond the most literal rendition of form and content must be dismissed out of hand as having no bearing to the true spirit of the artist and the values he either affirmed, over-determined or disempowered.

• • • • • •

With specific regard to the autonomy of value, Idries Shah instructs us thus in *Thinkers of the East* (Harmondsworth: Penguin, 1971)

i. The highly articulate of both the East and West have generally been in the grip of the belief that only a certain kind of organized thought can be used for learning. The fact is, however, that all the precedents, all the books, all the traditions which have produced the great thinkers of the past in the Orient show almost no trace of what is today believed to be organization (p. II).

ii. Rais El-Aflak, "The Lord of the Skies; who suddenly appeared in Afghanistan and then disappeared after giving a number of cryptic lectures, said:

Almost all the men who come and see me have strange imaginings about man. The strangest of these is the belief that they can progress only by improvement. Those who will understand me are those who realize that man is just as much in need of stripping off rigid accretions to reveal the knowing essence, as he is of adding anything.

'Man thinks always in terms of inclusion into a plan of people, teaching and ideas. Those who are really the wise know that the teaching may be carried out also by exclusion of those things which make man blind and deaf.' (p. 33)

iii. Ali said:

'None may arrive at the truth until he is able to think that the path itself may be wrong.

'This is because those who can only believe that it must be right are not believers, but peoples who are incapable of thinking otherwise than they already think. Such people are not men at all. Like animals they must follow certain beliefs, and during this time they cannot learn. Because they cannot be called "humanity", they cannot arrive at the truth.' (p. 38).

iv. Someone complained to a Sufi Sage that the stories which he gave out were interpreted in one way by some people and in other ways by others.

That is precisely their value, he said; "Surely you would not think much of even a cup out of which you could drink milk but not water, or a plate from which you could eat meat but not fruit? A cup and a plate are limited containers. How much more capable should language be to provide nutrition? The question is not "How many ways can I understand this, and why can I not see it in only one way?" The question is rather "Can this individual profit from what he is finding in the tales?" (p. 53)

Though Idries Shah, a leading interpreter of Sufism, compiled sayings and anecdotes dealing mainly with spiritual matters, their experiential disposition means for us that the value system suggested is in harmony with the totality of other life-forms as we know them.

• • • • • •

To compare Emile Zola and Balzac is to examine the trembling intercourse between values affirmed and values over-determined. Scholars have been quick to place Balzac's realism over Zola's perceived naturalism, seeing in the former a dynamic portrayal of life and reality and in the latter, a static, almost an illustrationist depiction of nature. To Georg Lukacs, for example, the three-dimensionality of reality is arrested in Zola's art in that while the examining force is active, the examined life appears sterile, stale and unmoving.

Yet, in the projection of existence, Zola remains a true interpreter of values, the affirmation of which emanates out of a life lacking in transcendence. The transcendental meaning of existence for Zola is the dilution and, ultimately, vulgarization of reality and conduct to the extent that that interpretation inexorably leads to intrusiveness and the assertion of a moral perspective. This assertion in turns opens up a complicated pattern of social articulation and discourse that either affirms, over-determines or disempowers values irrespective of, in fact, in utter disregard of a practical state of being.

For Balzac, on the other hand, the examination of life involves a transition of value into value; that is, the recourse to transcendental consciousness, not of the spirit, but as a fact of social life. While Zola affirmed values only, Balzac over-determines and disempowers values not as a response to social practice but as an over-affirmation of consciousness derived from moral imperatives. In attempting to add value to things, realities and experiences which are in themselves already possessed of value, he not only tinkered with the legitimacy of phenomena as they are (not as they ought to be), but also succeeds in imposing a state of suspended animation on the autonomous existence of those disempowered values as cogent, undeniable manifestations of life-forms.

It is true that there is cultural continuity in Balzac's dynamic social testimonies, yet this continuity is associated with the acute tension that characterizes all moral order, particularly those transformative and transmutative variants that search for universal acclaim. It is also true that the ingredient of social change is ingrained in Balzac's transcendental values, yet it is a change occasioned not by the loss of legitimate assertion by those values he disempowers but by two tendencies; his over-assertion of other contending values, and the creation of semi-autonomous values that exist between those that are over-determined and those that are de-asserted.

For Zola, life involves constancy free from the artefacts of social experience, if those artefacts are understood as unreal encrustations on experiences themselves. His sheer, pitiless, relentless and trenchant commitment to social truth may horrify the imagination but only to the extent that the consciousness is not violated by tendentious reflection but by the unwilling seduction of values as they are and not as we want them to be. He never crosses that trembling point relating to experiences in their essential contradiction, not because he is not capable of so doing, but primarily because he saw no reason to move beyond the point in which values are affirmed only.

Thus, the proper dividing line between Zola and Balzac, as two masters of life we must contend with, is that the one only affirmed values as life which exist as they are, while the other, in his assertion of social transition and cultural continuity, relatively over-determined and disempowered certain categories of values, and I derive my meaning from Earth and L'Assomoir **on the one hand, and** Cousin Bette and The Thirteen **on the other.**

● ● ● ● ● ●

Not many people realize (the few who do may not wish to acknowledge it) the close affinity between Mikhail Sholokhov and Boris Pasternak. Here, we not concerned with the surface, historical material on which the image-imperatives of their art was hinged: a Russian society caught between the tension occasioned by the transition of value (from Czarist autocracy to Revolutionary Bolshevism and the contradictions involved in that very succession in quantity and quality, including the red anger and the white backlash).

Now, we are concerned with a deeper kind of meaning and significance here, beyond the bland categorization of Pasternak as the anti-Soviet genius who celebrated the excesses of communism in *Dr. Zhivago* and Sholokhov, as the master of socialist realism, whose *And Quiet Flows the*

Don gave Soviet literary art its distinctive internationalist flair, clout, legitimacy and credibility; whereof its authenticity was achieved by his winning the Nobel prize in literature.

However, Pasternak and Sholokhov are one and the same in that in questioning and challenging the assumptions of their day, they granted each and every value its worth. They saw in life and reality the necessity of change, almost immanent, and virtually inexorable. Change in value; that is, the transition in nature is for them an objective occurrence whose dependence on basic laws and accident is ascertainable. The loyalty they owed to any given ideal is a loyalty reinforced by man's reflexive capacity; beyond this, they saw history as a moving engine of consciousness which attracts the values it wants to affirm and even over-determine and repels those other values it wishes to disempower.

It may even be realistic to assert that Sholokhov honoured more the spirit of the autonomous existence of values in *And Quiet Flows the Don* than Pasternak did in *Doctor Zhivago*. In the former, the consciousness of the artist is only directed towards the examination of the social forces which harbour various contradictory value attributes; the historical interplay of these forces in their search for assertion, affirmation and mastery; the objective process through which over-determination and disempowerment occur; and the near irreversible conditioning of emergent values in spite of, or rather in consideration of the values which are already sufficiently attenuated.

For Sholokhov, therefore, the reality of accentuation and attenuation of values is a by-product of a historical struggle; his sympathy for one over the other, as demonstrated later in *They Fought For Their Fatherland*, draws from a careful contemplation of a new historical reality which not only accorded well with his awareness of the meaning and significance of life and the nature of values it must carry but, more importantly, in the realization that the legitimacy of values depends, in the main, on the basis of their triumphal presence.

Pasternak virtually denounced this triumphal presence, in a half-intellectual, half-instinctual negation of the over-determining capacities of new socio-cultural and historical impulses. His conception of value and his cognition of man's estate on earth wear a carefully protected moral skein in that while he consistently rejected those historical and cultural imperatives which made the transition from value to value possible, he readily declared his commitment to an indeterminate humanistic philosophy whose properties may include poetry, love, fellow-feeling and compassion.

Pasternak's subjectivism is a hangover from a discriminating Christian ethical world order in that while he applauded man's innate freedom-cherishing capacities in his quest for perfection, he tried to impose a censorship on an emergent reality, no matter the materials and elements it carries. Pasternak's **Doctor Zhivago** is thus an excursion into the trembling relationship between an ideal state and reality as historically demonstrated; between man's inner spiritual yearnings and the de-spiritualized essence of his cultural milieu; between an incapacitated though adorable tradition and the excessive exuberance of a new system of value; and between an individual's relationship with a reality he codifies and an utterly aggressive social structure which, having been sufficiently asserted over other structures, is unmindful that over-determination inexorably leads to disempowerment, with all the incalculable damage that is done to the autonomy of value.

Thus, while Pasternak may appeal more to those who always seek for balance and the achievement of equilibrium, as intrusive as the adherence to their tenets is in relation to the free interplay between contending entities, Sholokhov surely appeals to those whose belief in the autonomy of all value forms is total and absolute in that he attempted a comprehensive objectification of the historical and cultural forces at work in nature without intrusiveness, with studied distance and calculated dispassion.

Sholokhov and Pasternak stand out as masters of culture in an era of change for they remain peerless in their investigation of the instincts that make strangeness appear ordinary, and of the convoluted patterns and processes whereby reality is impacted upon, transformed, and is either over-asserted or disempowered. Temperamentally, very little divides them except that to Pasternak, culture is a system of honourable relationships whose integrity is inviolate while to Sholokhov, culture is a mirror that records the changing patterns of beliefs and affirmations whose honour and integrity are by-products of the triumph of value over value or the transition from one cultural parameter to another.

Glimpses

The following extracts embody, in the main, the substance of Pasternak's cultivated instincts; in them is declared the essential ingredients of his understanding and assimilation of values and their autonomous and less than autonomous capacities. To this extent I believe (the idea first came to me in 1984) that *Doctor Zhivago* is not merely a strange type of aesthetic illumination but essentiality a cultural testament.

On History and Revolution

"History is not made by anyone. You cannot make history; nor can you see history, any more than you can watch the grass growing: Wars and Revolutions, Kings and Robespierres, are history's organic agents, its yeast. But revolutions are made by fanatical men of action with one track minds, men who are narrow-minded to the point of genius. They overturn the old order, in a few hours or days; the whole upheaval takes a few weeks or at most years, but for decades thereafter, for centuries, the spirit of narrowness which led to the upheaval is worshipped as holy."

Doctor Zhivago, p. 505.

On Contradictions in Value

"You grew up quite differently. There was the world of the suburb, of the railways, of the slums and tenements, dirt, hunger, over-crowding, the degradation of the worker as a human being, and the degradation of women. And there was the world of the mother's darlings, of smart students and rich merchant's sons; the world of impunity, of brazen, insolent vice; of rich men laughing or shrugging off the tears of the poor, the robbed, the insulted, the seduced; the reign of parasites whose only distinction was that they never troubled themselves about anything, never gave anything to the world and left nothing behind."

Doctor Zhivago, p. 498

On Tidal Waves

"I don't know if people will rise of themselves and advance spontaneously like a tide, or if everything will only be done in their name. Such a huge event cannot be asked for its credentials, it has no need to give dramatic proof of its existence, we'll take it on trust. It would be mean and petty to try to dig for the causes of titanic happenings. Indeed they haven't any. It's only in a family quarrel that there is a beginning - and after people have pulled each other's hair and smashed the crockery that they try to think who it was that started it. What is truly great is without beginning, like the universe. It confronts us suddenly as if it had always been there or as if it has dropped out of the sky."

Doctor Zhivago, pp. 201-202

On Incompleteness

"It turns out that those who inspired the revolution aren't at home in anything except change and turmoil: that's their natural element; they aren't happy with anything that's less than on a world scale. For them, transitional periods, worlds in the making, are an end in themselves. They aren't trained for anything else, they don't know about anything except that. And do you know why there is this incessant whirl of never-ending preparations? It's because they haven't any real capacities, they are ungifted. Man is born to live, not to prepare for life."

Doctor Zhivago, p. 328

• • • • • •

To understand the place of Dostoyevsky and Tolstoy in mankind's cultural history, with specific reference to either the affirmation, over-determination or disempowerment of values, we may need to consider the following samples:

Raskolnikov, a young student in *Crime and Punishment*, murders a grasping, old pawnbroker, a social and cultural "vermin", as it were, on the grounds of:

i. Assertion of will;
ii. Compassion for the poor; and
iii. Autonomous orientation of all values and perceptions.

However, he escapes the snare of the law but succumbs to the intimations of his conscience, becomes psychotic, delirious and distracted, is "saved" by a "fallen woman" and ultimately rejoices in the expectation of resurrection in penal servitude. Or Peter Verkhovensky, Stavrogin, Kirilov and the rest in *The Devils* whose grandiose plan of civil upheaval under an anarchist agenda becomes an unbearable moral burden out of which they sought exoneration in confession, self-recrimination and self-immolation. Such images endure in almost all his works, exception perhaps being *Notes From the Underground* and the character, Fyodor Karamazov in *The Brothers Karamazov*. Or consider Tolstoy's Anna Karenina *and* Resurrection (these value-carrying cultural capacities and incapacities do not come out quite forcefully in *War and Peace*, given the material he worked with, and the sheer, monumental scope of the recreated images). In the first, we witness a woman of substance who again

attempts to:
i. Exercise her will and thus;
ii. Establish the autonomous existence of value, particularly love and sex, but is made to accept the ascribed illegitimacy of her cultural freedom and commits suicide as a consequence of her social rejection. In the second, we are witnesses, again, to the fortunes of Prince Dmitri Ivanovich Nekhlyudov who blames himself for the "fallen womanhood" of Maslova, embarks on a mortifying journey of purification, as it were, and reconciles himself to the sanctity of the "moral" universe through self-attenuation.

Between Dostoyevsky and Tolstoy is the passionate, almost spiritual assertion of the will to life and existence, the legitimacy of forms of value and yet the over-determination and consequent disempowerment of different elements of culture. In probing the deepest layers of consciousness in order to ascertain the determinate components of motivation, both masters underlie the inescapable consequences of social and moral conduct. To this extent, they subscribe to the existence of a moral world order, and reject the revaluation of values that favours the authenticity of all life-forms. While Tolstoy may be more persuasive in his moral orthodoxy – readily declared with piercing insights in authorial commentaries – Dostoyevsky was no less a moralist who dissembled the balance that should exist in the contradiction between various value-forms.

Dostoyevsky and Tolstoy may have exhibited rebelliousness in their projection of image-imperatives; that is, the competence of man to assert the values from which he derives pleasure and satisfaction, yet they are masters of over-determination in not allowing all affirming values their proper legitimacy and cultural significance. This is to say that while they wished that life should be lived as an expression of innate desires, any desire, they were intolerant of those values that harbour the hidden capacity of dismantling established conventions and traditions. Tolstoy's over-affirmed disposition may have surpassed Dostoyevsky's earthy compassion for all lives (alcoholics, fallen women, nihilists, etc); however, in the full exploration of the necessity of change, the independent, autonomous existence of all life-forms and the transition from value to value, they stand on the same pedestal. That cultural platform is the imperative of continuity and the inviolate nature of determinate moral conditions which, in spite of its inherence in humanism, will nevertheless be over-asserted beyond all other cultural assumptions.

• • • • • •

Other Voices

Paul Kennedy's strength derives from the sheer weight of historical evidence at his command and disposal. I didn't appreciate how unoriginal he was until I re-read my high school West African history text, and here I am referring to Kennedy with regard to *The Rise and Fall of the Great Powers*. That 1965 text provides this illumination in relation to Kennedy's thesis:

> The process of imperial growth was often the extension by force under an able military leader of the imperium of a particular ethnic group over the rest of the surrounding country. Administration itself was of two levels, one dealing with the particular ethnic group and the other with the empire as a whole ... Ability to keep these diverse groups together therefore depended largely on the military resources of the empire and none of these empires really provided a solution to this problem.
> (1. F. Ade Ajayi & Ian Espie, eds. *A Thousand Years of West African History, p. 58,* Reference is to the Empires of the Western Sudan).

Paul Kennedy therefore stands out as a relentless assessor of mankind's historical progress and a dispassionate narrator of change and its consequences. To the extent that he remains an objective prism of conducts, one can say for him that he subscribes, though half-willingly, to the necessity of the autonomous existence of values. To Kennedy, the legitimacy of any historical 'value' (in his context, "powers") depends largely on its continual affirmation, and even over-determination of will; its inauthentic spirit derives from its incompetence to challenge and forestall those autonomous forces (internal and external) that seek to disempower it. The then Soviet Union provided Kennedy his legitimate claim to universal recognition; the future destiny of USA will establish his claim to greatness and immortality.

• • • • • •

While it may not be wholly correct to describe Edward Said as an advocate of liberal, humane causes, including the legitimacy of diverse cultural persuasions in a universe already over-determined by an imperial cultural monolith, there is no denying that he comes across as an intellectual caught between the distance that separates private discourse from public meaning and significance. Edward Said's originality stems from that rare human ability to differentiate between the instincts, impulses and perceptions that men and women carry within them, and which operate beyond the limits set by historical and cultural milieu–dependent practices and life-forms which inflict enormous damage to the autonomy of values.

It is in this regard that his passionate involvement in the great cultural debates of our time, particularly the construction of post-colonial theoretical platforms and the enunciation of the notion of independent centres of cultural affirmations (wherein true liberty could be achieved for all races, nations and people) with the cognition of the expansive role of the intellectual whose publics are diverse and contradictory, and whose viewpoints must be recognized and appreciated by genuine minds, that mark him out as a master of consciousness and cultivated instincts.

Edward Said's perceptual paradigm is such that from Orientalism, *Culture and Dependency* to *The Representations of the Intellectual,* he successfully masks his acclamations and declamations (he has contributed more to Palestinian causes than any other living person, at least on the issues of cultural identity and historical relevance) to the extent that his testaments stand today not as the declarations of a man with a restrictive historical and cultural inheritance, but as a sufficiently distantiated intellectual who regards the whole of humanity as his immediate constituency. It is precisely because his intellectual strategy involves going beyond the surface of the material at his command to capture the essential over-determination of some values and the consequent disempowerment of others, in order to create balance in the interpretations of cultures, that he achieves his significance as a master of consciousness and immortality as an original intellect.

• • • • • •

If Paul Kennedy is an objective assessor of historical reality and Edward Said an intellect confronted with, and continually resolving the contradiction between private meaning and the significance of wider publics, then Francis Fukuyama appears as the classic case of a mind that must settle all historical and philosophical contentions only on the basis of the over-determination of values. Fukuyama's historical, philosophical and political thesis does not only stem from its non-original paradigmatic structure:

i. Hegel's liberal humanism translated into Western liberal democracy, capitalism and free market practices which thus heralds the cessation of all historical processes; and
ii. Marx's absolutization of the process of historical

dialectics which translated into 20th century communism that lost out in the struggle with the first thesis.

Properly speaking, Fukuyama's fatal perceptual error is thus not in the art of borrowing, but in allowing himself to be entrapped in the false absolutist judgment about the nature, character, structure, endurance and significance of historical, political and ideological values.

In simple terms, Fukuyama's thesis in *The End of History and The Last Man* is that two great historical, political, philosophical and ideological tendencies have shaped the modern age: the liberal humanist paradigm of Hegel which has consequented into modern industrial, liberal democratic capitalist societies of the West, and Marx's dialectical and historical materialism which produced the communist societies of Europe, Asia and elsewhere; that our age has been a theatre of confrontation between these two tendencies in their quest for supremacy, assertion and over determination; that the disintegration of the Soviet Union and the dismantling of orthodox communist structures in Eastern Europe is the triumph of the Hegelian model over its Marxist counterpart; and that henceforth historical, ideological, political and philosophical thoughts will cease to procreate and mutate as mankind has arrived at the terminal point of its historical evolution whose end is liberal democracy, and the last man a liberal democratic capitalist.

It is of course an expression of cultural arrogance for segments of life-forms to be clothed with the aura of universal validity irrespective of the other independent, autonomously existing forms and values. This limited knowledge which is passed off as universal wisdom suffers from two debilitating handicaps: the non-recognition of values and over-determination of partially selective values that in turn implies the disempowerment of other values already recognized. Rephrased somewhat, what is being stressed is that by choosing just two models, paradigms or theses in the context of the existence of a multiplicity of other choices, Fukuyama fails to acknowledge the reality of the relegated values (non-recognition; the issue of legitimacy, authenticity and autonomy does not even arise for values are only legitimate or illegitimate, etc. on the basis of their primary recognition), and by over-determining liberal democracy at the expense of communism which is subsequently disempowered in an evolving transitional period whose ultimate end-result is presently unknown, he wreaks havoc on the autonomy of those values which he recognizes.

There is no doubt that Fukuyama is a relentless, confident and persuasive thinker whose ideas, in my mind, remain the most disturbing in the history of political thought for over a generation. But as thorough as his analysis is, and as detailed as his references are, he still fails on three vital scores: the non-recognition of values; the over-determination and disempowerment of recognized values; and the in-alertness to the legitimacy of all existing values, recognized or non-recognized. It is plainly on this last score that he repeats some of the misjudgements of Hegel and Marx; that is, that historical evolution, which is the struggle between various value-forms, is predictable; that this struggle will follow already, given and well regulated laws and patterns; and that the triumph of a particular value over another implies the cessation of historical processes.

Values will always exist in a self-contained and self-reinforced order, regardless of their status at any given historical era, and regardless, too, of the meaning and significance which they achieve for themselves at any point in time. While the over-determination of value may well serve the needs of "ultimate values" like death, it will surely not serve the purposes of values whose meaningfulness is relative, for the succession and supplanting of values will always occur in human existence as a testament of the infinite cycle of reality. This, to my mind, is the essential handicap of Fukuyama's otherwise brilliant intellect.

182 ■ AUTONOMY OF VALUES

• • • • • •

I find Ngugi's *Moving the Centre: The Struggle for Cultural Freedoms* a significant departure from his earlier intellectual productions. It is not just that he de-affirmed the class approach to issues of conflict of values in favour of the legitimacy of indeterminate national values which find expression in the inherent authenticity of a multiplicity of universal cultural centres, but also that his intellectual evolution has indicated a transition from the over-determination and disempowerment of values to the recognition of the autonomy of values. Thus, **Moving the Centre ...** is the purest expression of his intellectual strength in that he makes expansive allowance for the co-existence of several cultural centres, equal to themselves in status, meaning, relevance and significance, and free from the determinations of a restrictive class identity. This marks a departure from his earlier intellectual and artistic expressions that could be schematized thus:

i. The over-determination of non-class described national humanism and liberal democracy, with the consequent disempowerment of colonial imperialism (*The River Between, Weep Not Child, The Black Hermit, This Time Tomorrow* and *A Grain of Wheat*).
ii. The over-determination of class-described and class-contained national humanism (Marxist-liberationist paradigm which recognizes only the legitimacy of the proletarian class and the peasantry (*Petals of Blood, The Trial of Dedan Kimathi, Devil on the Cross, I Will Marry when I Want, Mother Sing For Me, Matigari, Home Coming, Writers in Politics*, and *Barrel of a Pen*); and
iii) Finally, his current thesis on the autonomy/legitimacy of national values and cultural practices which must, as a whole, be liberated from the over-determining cultural intolerance of the West; an idea first indicated in *Decolonizing the Mind* but subsequently elaborated and made more cogent in *Moving the Centre*.

MASTERS OF CONSCIOUSNESS ■ 183

Ngugi is my favourite African writer/intellectual (the most mentioned in all my works and writings), and this stems from a common attitude towards identity and consciousness; a common passion in affirming a viewpoint; a common commitment in arguing an issue; but most importantly in the uncanny appreciation of the fact that the revaluation of values, wherein their autonomous, independent existence is declared, is so much better for the health and freedom of mankind than the aggressive over-assertion and disempowerment of values with restrictive meaning and significance.

● ● ● ● ● ●

Need we be relative in our encomiums? Need we be squeamish in the use of superlative terms? We need not be. In apprehending the life-force of a Master of Consciousness, we must constantly declare our standpoint in absolute terms. The idea of relativity in underscoring human attributes is not only a concession to ignorance which guarantees intellectual "safeness", it is also cognitive deficiency that apprehends values only at their point of incarnation, determination and, maybe, affirmation. To understand that some life-forces have successfully crossed these thresholds to the dwelling place of over-empowerment, is to readily declare with relish that which has demonstrated the highest form of triumphal presence. Only the genius ever attains this peak, in spite of the harm these can and do inflict on the autonomy of values.

As a Master of Consciousness, we declare, without reluctance or hesitation, that Luciano Pavarotti was the greatest operatic tenor to have ever lived; that Michael Jackson is the greatest pop artist of all time; and Fela Anikulapo Kuti, the greatest musician Africa has ever spawned. All of them combined the elemental force of creativity with the mastery of instinctual conduct, breaking as they did, and with effortless ease, the boundaries of human materiality with the culture of transcendence, and bestriding, as immortals, the threshold of human reasoning and the inscrutable depth of our collective unconscious. For in their chosen craft, we can only but express that its nature, essence, range, evocative power and, need we say, form, can never be the same again, at least not in our lifetime.

Chapter

9

ILLUMINATION
(AN ACCOUNT OF A CONSCIOUS LIFE)

I

Song of Incarnation:
Njaa-aka-Njaa had a dream at the precise time nature weighed her balancing scale between light and darkness. Minus the flapping of the night bird, Ishirikpam, and the gentle belch of a distant thunder, an ethereal silence bathed the brooding forest. His hut was suspended above the tree branches, nearer the clouds than the gurgling stream down in the valley, farther from earth, yet distant from the sky. It was built on time-threshold; immaterial, incandescent, yet breathing with stilled animation. Its trance-like posture was belied by the vapour that poured through its roof, transfiguring into shapes, first of Njaa, then of Yatube, and finally of the headless trunk of Omanta. The trunk had a distended neck, out of which protruded a golden halo, full of stars and fireflies which illumined the vapour and the transfigured shapes.

Njaa woke with a start, scampered out of his raffia-mat, made for the fireplace and began to poke the crackling logs.

Sweat dripped off his body in rivulets, smarting his eyes, and in his mouth was the bitter taste of death. He felt presences all around him, more concrete than the beings that troubled his sleep. Not the presence of his disciples who lay in peaceful slumber all around them but the hurrying by of day, night, sun, the earth and the 3 planes of life he had already experienced in his whole existence.

As he squatted, poking the fire, he heard a gentle call through the low eaves, a running feet and a mocking laughter. He rushed to the wooden door, flung it open and saw that the vapour had vanished, his shape gone. With them went the earth on a distant journey. She did not beckon to the moon whose wailings roused the sun to fits of anger. It too departed from the heavens, with ash heaps for companion, and plucked feathers of a falcon clutched in his hands. A bright light appeared before his very eyes from the eastern horizon, then the earth settled amongst them again; the earth and all the dried streams and ponds.

His dream was not only full of these presences; he also saw a river of skulls, bones and blood, sluggish with age and burden, and naked people bathing just by its banks. He had called out to them to leave the blood, the bones and the skulls but received only hooting laments in return; a lamentation full of mockery. One by one they plunged into the river of blood, became fishes of all sizes, and began to swim to the depths. He also saw a raging fire, heard the cries of forest animals and hordes of hunters with guns, rockets and bazookas. The ashes melted with a ferocious speed and green shrubs sprouted from the earth. The hunters laid down their weapons, gathered the sprouting leaves and wore them as clothes.

In the afternoon, he gathered his followers under a large Iroko tree at the centre of the town square and began to instruct them as follows:

- Nature manifests its consciousness of being in a variety of ways. It is a product of its own self-incarnation, and thereafter proceeds to procreate other life-forms. The earth, the sun, the moon, the sky, the stars and the clouds are governed by laws which only nature harbours. Their own consciousness of self is already pre-determined and regulated by binding laws which are generated only by nature. Man also is a primary product of nature, and because he achieves the highest level of affirmation after incarnation, is well poised to master his own source of being.

- I may now reveal the meaning of my dream to you. The hut we dwell in is suspended between all the layers of existence; that is nature. It has a foothold on earth, because we the dwellers are anchored deep on the world of matter. It reaches out to the sky and the clouds because we always yearn for transcendence and eternity. Between the material world and the world of our transcendental yearnings are regions of transfigurations, vapours and mists. They assume concrete shapes, and also indeterminate shapes; they are the occult zones of experiencing, for while we wear the shape in which we are in now, we desire a change of our status because of our persistent yearning for immortality. This change conditions our transitional behaviour in that we appear different from ourselves when that yearning becomes an obsession ...
- The river that flows with blood, bones and skulls is both the river of life and death, for nature incarnates both states of existence. Because nature is in itself a self-transforming entity, man, its primary product, equally harbours this capacity. The change he undergoes and the new status he attains ensure for him a measure of belonging to and identification with the world of matter and the world of transcendence, and for those who are truly evolved their consciousness is without limit, like those who have experienced all the 3 planes of existence.
- Culture is nature's breathing-valve, and like her, is timeless in dimension. Culture is the concrete manifestation of nature as value, and because nature

realizes itself as a process, so does culture reject the force of history and change, except on the basis of struggle between autonomously incarnated values. This resistance is not a negation of tradition and change, but recognition of the validity of all cultural forces that are codified by nature at the cradle of incarnation.

- Man is a cultural product. Therefore, man, like I said, is the engine of nature, the source of its self-awareness. This being so, all the relationships man establishes with other men, with the objects of culture, and with nature itself, are legitimate relationships notwithstanding the nature of cultural consciousness that a particular historical epoch affirms and over-determines.

When Njaa paused in his declarations, a fierce wind rose up, apparently from nowhere. The wind turned into a gale, a hurricane, a blizzard and a tornado. Monsoon rain poured down in torrents and all around the seated disciplines rivers ran deep and wide. Then the sun appeared which dried their drenched clothes and caused the rivers to flow thin. The sun was followed by the appearance of night, the bellow of a thousand thunders and the dazzling brilliance of innumerable lightning. The sky became full of stars, at the centre of which was a radiant moon.

Njaa looked up to the sky and spread his hands over the heads of his seated disciplines. Night soon gave way to an indeterminate, ethereal light, full of rainbow shadows. On the first colour were the surging mists and vapours. On the second was the river of blood, bones and skulls. On the third was the sun, the stars and the moon. On the fourth were the winds, the gales and the tornadoes. On the fifth they saw the rumbling of earthquakes and volcanoes. On the sixth was darkness and brooding silence. And on the seventh was the face of a man, a woman, a child, a bird, a fly, an ant, a leopard and a green leaf.

- What does all this mean, master, one of his disciples asked in a quaking voice.

- My child, Njaa answered him gently. You are witnesses to the birth of life and existence. You are all participants in the song of incarnation. Nature is as multitudinous as the sands of the ocean. Each particular has a life of its own; its entity a form of its unique incarnation. The value we attach to life, and the values that nature produces are autonomous values for they obey no other law other than the recognition of their own essence as forms of life. They pose no danger to other forms of life except in the process of interaction. When they interact, they begin to affirm and assert themselves, sometimes in recognition of the pre-determined will of other life-forms; at other times in utter denial of their very existence. Man expresses this tendency at its highest level, for the mastery he seeks over nature, and the mastery that the ruling castes seek, is only in the justification of man's legitimate existence. This never can and never will invalidate the consciousness, self-declared and sometimes self-objugating, existence of other products of nature.

• • • • • •

Beware Of What You Believe!

Njaa's disciples were seated around him inside an uncompleted shopping mall in the heart of a large modern city. High above them the workmen were hammering away on the scaffold. Traffic roared past them, and on all the side streets around the mall (it was being built near a major road intersection), they could hear the sounds and murmurs of the city. Yet, the large warehouse area they were seated in was pervaded with a deep silence; the silence of serenity and solitude. They felt very deeply about their presence in the city, to which they had journeyed for seven days. At the same time, they felt far removed from the reality around, absorbed as they were with their inner thoughts, feelings and sensations.

- Beware of what you believe, Njaa instructed them. Belief is a prodigal child of nature, and like all prodigal children, is difficult to master. Though all manners of belief must in the end establish their connectedness with material reality, at their immediate point of affirmation, they tend to reject this affinity. Belief is a product of culture, but rejects all of culture as a whole, selecting for itself those cultural instincts which aid its exercise of prodigality. Belief cannot be separated from faith for in the latter does it seek to anchor all its cultural illusions. Do not believe things because you are in the habit of believing them, or because you are told to believe in them. Belief may bear the stamp of truth, not of all values, but of those values which aid it. Yet, belief is far away from fact because it builds its castle in its absence.
- Do not be partial in the selection of fact; for only truth is partial in its selection of details. Fact is a cultural necessity; truth is a transcendental illusion. Because faith is lacking where fact is present, all believers of a faith reject facts which exist outside the context of their belief. Be mindful that what you utter counts very much regarding what you believe, because the fact of life, the fact of existence, and the fact of experience, all are equal to themselves and occupy the same autonomous plane in the incarnation of values.
- I give you just two examples. You are always told to be the best of what you are, meaning that you must affirm your possibility or potentiality to its fullest degree. This statement in itself has a basis on fact; it selects nothing, and rejects nothing. However, your cultural conditioning does not allow for the full exploitation of this valid, factual and non-selective cultural experience, for in being the best of what you are, you are only being told to accept a moral truth and not a cultural fact. You are told (if is implied) that you should be the best corporate strategist, aeronautics engineer, university professor and a member of parliament. You are told (it is implied), not

to be the best insider trader in a stock market, a first-class prostitute or pimp, an insurance fraudster, a contract assassin, the best rapist around or the most distinguished serial killer in town. Yet, all these things are products of culture, and people do indeed aspire to be the best in them.

To be the best of what you are is, culturally, to be the best of anything in life. To separate the vocations of life into what is worthwhile and morally elevating and what is worthless and morally reprehensible is to cross a discernible cultural boundary: it is to transit, via ethnical distance, from fact to truth, from reality to belief, and from experience to faith. This transition renders culture meaningless for it codifies all its energies into a tiny prism of discriminatory social consciousness, and in doing that violates the sanctity of all autonomously incarnated values by over-determining certain cultural forces over others. The only way you can justify belief is by a factual demonstration of the unique autonomous incarnation of what you believe in as against the secondary, reactive incarnation of those other rejected life-forms. Until you do this successfully, always be wary of the badge of faith you carry, any faith indeed, and always beware of the belief system that seduces you, any belief system for that matter.

- The next example I give you is very close to the first. People always tell you about their destined role in life in so far as such a role is culturally acceptable in their environment. You are warned not to run against the current of destiny as this may be physically, socially, professionally and spiritually harmful, but to discover that destiny (talent) early enough and build on it. A precocious child who is a mathematical prodigy turns out later in life to be a computer whizkid. This is destiny. A grade 11 sprinter becomes an Olympic gold medalist. This also is destiny. A grade 10 class orator becomes a successful politician, a charismatic national figure. That too is destiny. Not so, the child who touches the opposite sex in their 'private parts' at age 10, who later becomes a child molester and a serial killer. Not so, too, a 9-year-old who pilfers his classmates' pencils and erasers and turns out into an armed robber, and not so a 12-year-old girl who loves the company of older boys and who becomes in adult life a craver of "forbidden" sexual passion and pleasures.

- The belief in destiny without pre-destination is a cultural fallacy. It rejects the idea of God as a transcendental cultural force who wields the limitless or infinite capacities that man yearns for but cannot materially achieve. The belief in destiny with pre-destination is a cultural illusion because it creates the cultural image of a Godhead who is partial and unjust in the conferment of talents, particularly culturally sanctified talents. Such a belief is a concession to divine self-knowledge, for if God is the author of all existence, and before all and every material incarnation of human life, has not only apportioned a prescribed destiny but equally is a witness to future death (under any context), then man stands absolved of all cultural and ethical blames in the exercise of his pre-destined material role and fate in life.

Destiny is but a cultural barometer which measures the behaviour of cultural forces in any determinate cultural milieu. Destiny is, thus, a cultural fact, if and only if it accommodates all life-forms within its integral dynamics. Destiny becomes the truth of a culture if it separates values into moral segments, as truth is very far away from the real experience of culture. Here, again, I must warn you: do not be hasty in judging others' manifest destiny for in doing so, you would have been ensnared in the trap set by time and space. Always guard against the classification of cultural practices as good or evil because you must please the present-day custodians of cultural and ethical norms. All manifest destiny, just like all manifest belief, stand in equality to themselves on the basis of cultural fact. To prove otherwise the reality of this thesis is to search out all those values (destinies) which enjoy original incarnation and all those others which enjoy secondary or reactive incarnation. When you do this, search out also the pattern of struggle between all values and all life-forms, and the stages cultural transition undergoes before a discriminatory cultural and moral world order succeeded in creating a distance, through over-determining and dis-empowering strategies, between all facts of culture and acceptable cultural truths. Until you do this, regard destiny as a cultural illusion, and all manifest talents as imperishable cultural facts.

Just as Njaa finished speaking, and before any of his disciples had time to ask him a question or make any observation, they heard a loud curse outside the shopping mall; a curse and a bellow of deep-throated anger which was followed by a swish of what sounded like leather on a human body. The angry roar was followed by a piercing, piteous scream of a small girl whose patter as she ran belied the extreme desperate situation she was in. Njaa went outside the warehouse and saw a confounding spectacle before his eyes. A ragged, poorly clothed girl, with dishevelled hair, tears streaming down her pinched face, was running as fast as she could. Closely following her was a short, squat, grim-faced man who clutched a leather dog leash with which he was pounding the girl as she ran. The young girl, probably 13 years of age, saw Njaa at the entrance to the warehouse, seemed to gain strength from his welcoming posture, ran over the gutter and buried her head on his chest, her arms reaching out to him for refuge and support.

The grim-faced man paused just before the gutter, glared at Njaa who looked back at him in sympathy. His resolve seemed to have failed him for he only muttered; "Never you set your illegitimate feet in my house, you bastard hussy. The next time I see you in the neighbourhood, the vultures will have a feast". With that he spat inside the gutter, turned round and strode away. Njaa led the young girl inside the warehouse, wiped her face and her nose, ruffled her hair tenderly and made her sit amongst his disciples.

Upon gentle prodding, Njaa and his disciples learnt that the little girl, who gave her name as Angel, was born out of wedlock. Her mother ran away from home at the age of 16 to escape the beatings and torture from the hands of an abusive father. Her grandmother was an alcoholic. Her mother became homeless, soon fell under the spell of a motor-cycle gang leader, became pregnant and begot Angel when she was seventeen. Angel's mother eventually got a job as a bartender in a low-class restaurant and moved into a small, shabby room of her own. It was there that Angel was brought up. Though life was hard and often depressing and gloomy they managed as best as they could.

Her mother got tired of looking after herself and three months ago married a local teamsters' union leader – the man who was chasing her down the street. From the start, he made it clear to her that he didn't want a "bastard" in his house and beat and abused her as often as he could. Her mother lacked the moral resolve to leave her husband and life became really menacing for Angel. The cause of her present travails, she said, was that she went on a picnic with some friends about 12 noon that day and came back around 4 p.m. in the evening. Now she has no place to go because, according to her, she would rather take her own life than be subjected to any other further debasement in their house. She concluded that her stepfather's insensate anger against bastards never stopped him from eyeing her lustfully, sticking his hands under her pants and fondling her breasts ...

There was a heavy silence in the warehouse after Angel's narration, apart from the discernible roar of city traffic and the murmur of city-dwellers walking on the sidewalks. Njaa bowed his head for a few minutes and then looked up to face his disciples, a faraway look in his eyes. He then proceeded to instruct them as follows:

- Beware, again, my dear ones, about what you hear, what you see and what you believe. This suffering child here is a gift of nature, and like nature has purity, which is self-declaratory. Her life has a value, and does not need other cultural forces to make it valid. Her birth is a product of a union between two cultural forces; that of man and that of woman. This in itself is a sufficient testimony of her being and existence. And like other forms of existence whose incarnation is an end-result of a conscious design, she stands as a testament of the fact of culture as against the truth of morality or religion.
  In man's original cultural presence on earth, the self-willing union of two or more individuals is a requisite ground for procreation and re-procreation of the human stock; latter-day cultural injunctions and socially binding relationships are but forms of corruption and distortion of the autonomy of this original cultural testament. To the extent that they are cultural irritations they add no extra value to the process of procreation and achieve no recognition as a structure of cultural self-realization.
- Beware of false testimonies about birth, marriage and illegitimate children. All births are a natural process of incarnating values; all marriages, provided that they pose no harm to this original incarnation of value, could well be tolerated as a valid expression of cultural progress. All products of nature stand in equal relationship to another, more so, birth which is the most sublime manifestation of cultural renewal. Man does not procreate the way the birds of the air, the animals of the forest or the fish of the water do, simply because he is a cultural pretender. In his free, liberated cultural state, man may yet learn some lessons from these other

forms of life. Today, man is on the threshold of that discovery because through cloning the cultural illusion of illegitimate birth or bastard children will be laid to a permanent rest.

- Beware particularly of the kind of marriage you will lend yourself to. Marriages based on social contracts and religious rites are relationships that make exaggerated concessions to man's cultural slavery for in them do we witness the most excessive form of over-determination of value via the pre-determination of the validity of such arrangements by the ruling cultural and religious caste. While the union between man and woman, without ethical, social or religious compulsion, (which pretends to add additional value to life) is a legitimate sell-expression of mankind's original cultural existence, the pre-determined and socially sanctioned union between man and woman is nothing but the dis-empowerment of this original cultural state.
- I therefore hasten to admonish you as follows: Do not look down on your fellow man because he is not conceived in the very image you desire, image which is determined by your own pattern of conception, wherein is reposed your belief. To do so is to inflict an enormous harm to man's constant search for cultural liberty and his persistent quest for affinity with nature.
- Do not question the legitimacy of the union between two individuals on the basis that such a union has not been sanctified by either religion or existing social mores. To do so will imply that they lack wisdom in their free choice, with the consequence that you deny people their natural ability to affirm the values which give them joy, happiness and peace of mind.
- Never be in the habit of calling anybody a bastard or an illegitimate person for wedlock exists the instant two or more people decide to live together, procreate together, for such a task, if it may be so-called, aids one of the most basic meanings of existence: the

perpetuation of the human stock.
- All marriages are false relationships in so far as their ultimate purpose is the denial of individuals their fundamental right of free cultural union, in so far as the compel individuals to act against their objective cultural interests and instincts; and in so far as the bonds they create do not aim at satisfying the natural desires of individuals, but in maintaining the unjust religious and cultural establishment manipulated by a ruling religious and cultural clique. To this extent, I can even instruct you that weighed on the scale of validity, the products of this kind of union are more illegitimate in the cultural sense of the term for they owe their incarnation, not on the basis of the fusion between two autonomous cultural entities, but on the specific demand of a reactive, secondary incarnation of a determinate cultural value.
- Finally, I say to you, do not believe in anything because others believe in it; do not castigate anything because others castigate it; do not condemn anything because others condemn it; and do not applaud anything because others applaud it. Weigh your belief against the evidence of ascertainable cultural fact, and if the fact is transcendental in nature, examine its relationship with the material properties of nature. Nature never revolts against itself; it never can, whether in the area of matter, consciousness or transcendence. Nature rather gathers all her children to her timeless bosom, protects them with passion and jealousy, and by so doing separates her products from the products of her products. This, I say to you, for belief is not a direct product of nature, but the product of nature's product.

Having instructed them thus, Njaa led Angel by the arm and, with his disciples walking behind him, walked out of the warehouse into the rapidly gathering dusk which the glitter of city lights fought in vain to stave off.

• • • • • •

The Power to Heal

They had not covered more than one kilometre when Angel developed a serious fever. Njaa noticed that her steps lacked their confident strides which impressed him when they set out from the warehouse. He felt a burning sensation in his hand which held her wrist and looked down to observe her face closely. He could see that her breathing was laboured, and that she was making a desperate effort to mask her pain.

He looked over his shoulder and saw a huge neon light indicating the presence of a general hospital nearby. He led her and his disciples through the cobbled pathway and was soon ringing the door-post bell. The nurse that came out took just one look at Angel and virtually carried her to a couch. Before long a wheeled bed was deposited before her and she was whisked out of sight. The surprising thing was that nobody seemed to take notice of Njaa's presence at the emergency ward. Doctors on duty were summoned, and together with very efficient nurses, bustled about to save her young life. Breathing apparatus were hooked over her nose. She was put on drip and intravenous injections were administered.

Angel was discharged the following day, as hearty as the sunlight itself. She sang happily as the party continued their journey. However, on the seventh day, her fever returned with a vengeance and she literally collapsed into Njaa's arms. He could not really feel her pulse, and her breathing came in thin, scratchy jerks. They were now inside a dense forest, with only a light glowing at the far distance. They hurried to the light and came face to face with a hut with raffia leaf roof. Sitting on a tree trunk in front of the house was a wizened old man who sat motionless, as if in contemplation of another life. Njaa laid Angel on the mat spread in front of the old man and narrated to him the story of Angel's health travails.

The old man nodded silently, got up with difficulty and entered his low hut. He came out after a fairly long time (Njaa's disciples were already losing their patience and were beginning to mutter and murmur) with a few odds and ends. He sat down again on the tree trunk, beat his metal gong, rattled some stringed shells and rolled lumps of limestone on the ground. He did this three times, then picking a bunch of leaves from an earthenware gourd he came out with, began to chew it. He masticated slowly, and then spat the whole sodden mess over Angel's face. He brought out a black ointment from a green bottle and began to rub it all over her body. Angel spluttered, heaved up and began to vomit. The old man got up from the trunk again, fetched water in another earthenware gourd and washed her face. Then he gave her a little of the ointment to drink.

- My children, the old man said, you can take her with you. Go in peace. She has been released from the bond of fear. She will be sick no more.
  Njaa thanked him, paid him some money and departed with Angel and his disciples. It was on the second month after this encounter that one of his disciples, who had taken a particular interest in Angel's health, endeavoured to ask him:
- Master, what we witnessed recently is most unusual. We are always led to believe that modern medicine is the most effective, safe and scientifically proven method of curing diseases and treating sicknesses. Yet, that medical practice failed Angel, who was subsequently cured by a medical practice which our age disapproves of, and which is sometimes condescendingly called "alternative medicine". Why is this so?

To this Njaa said to them:
- I say to you today, and I speak of all times, you will

never know the full meaning of life, unless you have experienced much of it. What you know is the product of the state of your being; it is conditioned by your consciousness, sense of perception, and sometimes, instinctual aura and cognitive sensation. No life-form is superior to another, and in medical practice, this is even more so. There is little sense in the separation of medical practice into orthodox or alternative, or modern and traditional. All medical practices are orthodox in themselves, alternative to one another and modern and traditional from the point of view of culture.

The primary purpose of medicine is to save lives, enable man live a healthy life, and heal the diseases that afflict the human race. If any system of medical practice achieves these objectives, it establishes its close affinity with nature, and the culture that nature incarnates. If it fails to do this, it creates a distance between a specific cultural need of man (a healthy life) and the structure of its realization. To that extent, it has failed in its cultural obligation.

The medical practice popular in the Western world, and which is becoming increasingly popular, too, in other parts of the world, stands in equality to other determinate medical practices which concede no recognition to this medical practice. It may be the Chinese system of acupuncture, the African dexterity with roots, herbs, and barks of trees, or faith healing by Pentecostal churches, or parapsychology and other psychic therapies. The list is endless. What they all aim to achieve is man's state of cultural perfection through individual and collective healthy existence. Sometimes, they achieve this; at other times, they fail to do so. The degree to which any medical practice does this is dependent not on the practice itself, but on the competence of the practitioners.

- I say to you, now, and for all times, the present cultural arrogance of the Western world which is expressed in its medical practice is nothing but a concession to ignorance. This ignorance has stifled Western intellectual thought and scientific advances by confining them to a pre-determined elementary definition and understanding of nature and the forces that shape it. The primary causative agent of this cultural blindness is Western material attainments which is made coterminous with other forms of cultural attainments.

When this blind cultural ignorance is successfully challenged, say by a telekinetic agent, a parapsychologist, an Indian guru or a Tibetan lama, a sense of bafflement occurs. Such ignorant men then scamper to their libraries and laboratories and re-emerge with torturous theses about new wisdom and new found knowledge. Grudgingly, they concede the reality of these other cultural forces, give them new names and, condescendingly, tolerate them as alternative medical practices.

- Medical history has no cultural image; neither does it recognize cultural motions. It only serves as a barometer of cultural awareness of needs at determinate historical periods. This is so because the essence of medical practice is the healing of the sick, and any such practice which so achieves this object is as modem as the latest computer no matter its age in use or the procedure it adopts. Medical practice has no age; its age is measured only by its efficacy. It has no age, too, for its primary concern, the cure for the sick, recognizes no historical age also.

- Angel was not healed by the doctors in the city not because their medical practice is not efficacious but because they applied the wrong medicine to the wrong ailment. Had they done otherwise, she would have been cured. Their medical knowledge, I must stress, is limited by a clear cultural fact: the experience open to them, and the experience they have thus far encountered. The old man healed her, for he understood her ailment and applied the right treatment. Between the two practices stands the icon of knowledge and experience. Between them also stands the reality of two autonomous, but related life-forms equal to themselves, and equal in affirmation, notwithstanding the cultural ignorance – turned arrogance – that I spoke of ...

Having instructed them thus, Njaa led them away from the forest, over the plains, and to the mountain-top where they will retire for the night.

• • • • • •

The 3 Planes of Existence

Njaa sat with Angel and his disciples on the mountain-top. Far below the earth was spread out like a well laid out lawn. The trees on the mountain sides moved gently with the wind, occasionally sighing in contentment on the caressing touch of nature's own product. The river below was very still, though periodically its motionless state was ruffled by darting fish and rolling waves.

Up above, the sky was star-studded. A full moon appeared out of the scudding clouds, and as Njaa gazed up intently, the clouds now wore the shape of a man and, at other times, the shapes of an animal, a tree or a building. A shooting-star sped out of the eastern horizon across the whole expanse of the sky before extinguishing its light on the west. In the distance a thunder rumbled mightily and was quickly followed by the dazzling radiance of innumerable lightning. A light drizzle of rain pelted down on the mountain-top and all around the men the earth was wrapped in ethereal suspense, stillness and gloom.

Njaa ended his contemplation, and in response to the questioning looks of his disciples and the strange fear he saw in Angel's eyes, said to them as follows:

- The quality of life does not derive from how fully you express a consciousness of a particular plane of existence, but to what extent you have mastered all the 3 planes of reality. I can tell you that nature creates a distance between its manifest auras, yet it constantly mediates between one aura and another. To master nature is to establish a connection between these 3 layers, not by sensory projection but only through experiencing. This is so because while sensory projection celebrates man's innate intellectual capacity of rationalizing the existence of these 3 planes, only instinct nourished over a lifetime of living can provide practical answers about the totality of nature's awareness of self.
- I have lived these 3 lives and lived them well. You who are with me today may not know this, for you see before you the outward appearance of a man whose birth you can narrate. What you may never know are those other intimations of an earlier existence, at the cradle of nature's self-incarnation. That life is lost to you for you do not see it in the trees that breathe, the river that weeps and the mountains that rumble. I see them clearly because I too was part of their life-force, part of their being and energy; I too was once a tree, a river and a mountain. This, if you must know, is nature's first plane of existence, a plane where values are sovereign, independent and autonomous, knowing only the awareness of self, and not recognizing the reality of other selves.
- You see me as a man today, but my presence before you is my second coming to earth for when I clutched the vapours and the mists that floated out of nature, like her, I became transcendent and free-floating, separating my body from myself, my life-force from any material bonds. This is the third plane of nature, the second, like I intimated you, being the existence you are presently witness to.

- Between these 3 planes are regions of affirmations, over-determination and mediations. Their forms of incarnation and re-incarnation are as diverse as the stars, known only to those who have lived them and have journeyed back to you, and those who are still experiencing them, before they show their second material presence.
- To affirm a value is to discover the potency of your consciousness, your being, and your reality. To over-determine a value is to cross cultural boundaries of belief and faith, and to declare that you alone matter in nature's ordering of reality. To disembody a value is to arrogate to yourself the power of the Godhead, to declare the immutability of your life-choice and the total invalidity of other life-choices.
- Those who have mastered the 3 planes of life are self-effacing in the conduct of their affairs, for like their source of incarnation, they know the havoc their strength and energy can wreak on half-conscious lives. These engines of nature's transcendental self-realization do not take for granted the power of out-of-body experiences, extra-sensory perception, soul-travel and tele or psycho-kinesis. To do so would entail the playing of God beyond the reaches of rational judgement and, through that, to disempower nature itself which created these transcendental substances.
- The 3 planes of life are but one in substance but not in form. The essence of nature as a pure state is the necessary condition for the liberty of its incarnated products; the essence of nature as man's material image is the necessary justification of cultural progress; and the essence of nature as a transcendental reality is the occult zone of experience in which total cultural freedom is yet possible on the absence of a Godhead. However, the significance of the Godhead may well be the victory of nature's over-lapping glory if such an image is seen as a 'de-moralized' incarnation of cultural

consciousness.
- Why do I tell you all these things today? I do so because you still have a whole life ahead of you, you still have layers of consciousness to explore, you still have to experience nature the way I have done. Soon, I will depart from your midst and embark on a long delayed journey. When I do so you will see the signs of my presence all around you; what you may not see are these other signs which nature hides from those who seek to corrupt her.
- I end my words to you now with the following declaration; never believe those who separate material life from spiritual life for they separate nature against herself. Never believe those who claim that existence has more than 3 planes, for they merely delude themselves about nature's form, not its substance. And never be in the company of those who overreach themselves through over-determination of reality for they are against nature's greatest gift: the autonomy of all values.

Having instructed them thus, Njaa led the way down through a narrow, rocky path towards the valley below. They came to the glittering water, sipped a little of its nourishing essence, and sat on the river bank, watching its clear, gentle flow.

• • • • • •

Searching For Heroes

Njaa and his disciples were approaching a fairly large settlement on the fringe of a desert. They could see from the distance, as far as the simmering rays of the midday sun which danced on the sand could allow, a cluster of mud houses with thatched roofs, and men and women, children and domestic animals, moving about. Very close to the settlement the little band saw a very old woman bent with age, who hobbled towards them on a walking-stick which she clutched in her trembling, withered hands. Njaa paused in front of her, and the rest stood behind him.

- Tell me, Mother, he addressed the old woman, is it possible for us to meet a hero in this settlement? We have searched far and wide; we have asked the same question among the mountain people, the river people, the city people and the forest people. They all seemed perplexed with our simple, honest quest, and could not give an answer that satisfied our curiosity. We are of the view that the condition of your existence in this blasted desert is such that will produce so many heroes.
- My son, the old woman replied in a quaking voice, you search in vain. What we have today are clowns and comedians who order our simple lives, who offer prayers to the Almighty, who settle local disputes, and who ensure that we have enough to eat even in the fiercest of droughts. Heroes are no more, for they were those daring men who protected the fair ladies from harm, who expanded the frontiers of our settlement with blood and destruction, and who rushed into wars without any consideration for their personal safety. Now that they are gone, we only sing to their blessed memory for the poetry in our hearts came from their mighty deeds. Heroes went with the wars; now that we have peace, heroes no longer live amongst us.
- Thank you Mother, Njaa answered her, you have instructed us well. Farewell.

  With that they departed from the settlement and went in search of an oasis, finding which they quenched their thirst and sat still at its bank.
- Though we have been searching for months now, asking in places far and wide and confronting all sorts of people for just a sign of what we seek, dear master, one of Njaa's disciples asked him after a while, how come it has been very difficult for us to seek out just a single hero among our today's leaders, and who, if it may please you to tell us, is a hero?

- To this Njaa made the following response: I have never encountered a worthier truth in all our wanderings and quests regarding that which we seek greater than the wisdom that came out of that old woman's mouth. Listen to me carefully that you may learn something new, and listen attentively for the logic in my words for he who is hard of hearing will later murmur that Njaa is in the habit of contradicting himself.
- To search for a real hero is to separate the clowns from the serious actors on the stage of life. And to discover him is to understand how several of nature's laws are broken. A real hero breaks the pattern of nature's self-affirmation and, to achieve heroism, he destroys the autonomous basis of a culture's advancement. This is so because heroism is a structure of over-determined values which prefigure the disempowerment of all unacceptable life-forms. A hero is thus an iconoclast, a breaker of nature's sovereign image after his self-declared will. Yet, we tolerate him in that in so doing, and in spite of the havoc he wreaks on the validity of these life-forms, he remains a serious cultural subject whose deeds and conducts may well carry society to a new theatre of awareness.

  But a clown also breaks nature's cycle of renewal and equally inflicts enormous harm on the autonomy of existing values. While he may be the leader of a religious, political or moral band, he is incapable of saying something new, interested as he always is, with the vacuous repetition of known cultural facts. Between these two dissembling cultural tendencies, we accept as genuine, the over-determining instincts of the serious actor and reject the comic irritation of the stage clown.
- Heroes achieve their greatest triumphal presence and originality in times of extreme strife. Through chaos and disorder, they seek out a pattern of cultural consciousness and urgency and end up imposing their

will on the reality at hand. Clowns are leaders in times of peace. They only serve as the regulating valve of cultural lethargy and all their efforts to build a new cultural milieu evaporate even before they start, for they have little or no wars to fight. The wars they create are a pale image of the real stuff, that is why they are always unconvincing when they embark on such clownish adventures, realizing instinctively that their greatness can only emerge out of the chaos and disorder that their mutative world rejects.

- Heroes are statesmen to the core; clowns are state technicians and tradesmen. Like cobblers, they can assemble a shoe, but they cannot create the materials for the shoe. Heroes are men like Alexander the Great who died of boredom because he had no new empires and lands to conquer. Heroes are like Julius Caesar who changed the republican face of Rome into an imperial monarchy and died as a result of that attempt. Heroes are men made of the stuff of Napoleon Bonaparte and Otto von Bismarck; great empire builders who altered the structure, the consciousness and the being of their states and their people. Heroes are men like Shaka Zulu who created a new Zulu monolith out of the disparate entities and kingdoms that previously owed allegiance to no other entity other than themselves. Heroes are the Lenins, Stalins, the Churchhills and the Roosevelts of the modern age, not in terms of our standpoint on their historical performance, but based on our understanding of what that term entails in history and culture.
- In our today's world, I can think of just a few heroes left. I can think of George Bush, though his heroism – as a consequence of the collapse of the Soviet Union and the retreat of Euro Communism which he didn't fight for, but rather inherited – is of a suspicious kind. He started as a technician but achieved a measure of heroism before he quit the political stage. The other

heroes of our time are Fidel Castro of Cuba and Nelson Mandela of South Africa.

Apart from these two figures the other leaders of our age are clowning stage hands and imitative state technicians who play an allotted role, in spite of their noise and exuberance, on a historical and cultural stage that is not of their making or creation.

- Beware of false leaders and false heroes for those who dance in the arena today do not understand the meaning of heroism and unlike the real heroes of all ages, they cannot be forgiven the damage they inflict on the autonomy of values.

Having spoken thus to them, Njaa led them away from the oasis and the desert into the gathering dusk to a totally different part of the world.

• • • • • • •

Till I Return, Beware of the Takers of Life

- I shall soon depart from you in my physical form, Njaa told his disciples, but my essence shall always be with you; instructing you about the mysteries of life and guiding your very steps as you strive to attain life's 3 planes. I shall always watch over you even as you labour daily to understand the real meaning of existence, separating as you do so, the inner rot that has become today's culture, from the original spirit of nature. Yes, for nature has its original, legitimate spirit: the exercise of free will accorded to all life-forms as they clash and mutate, and in their recognition and non-recognition of all manners of cultural presences, including theirs.
- v Before I depart from your midst, I leave you with not a moral burden, but a cultural dilemma. Every life-form has a right to life, once its presence is declared after incarnation; every cultural value is an essence of nature if it meets its productive requirement. To take a

life is to justify its non-productiveness; and if this criterion is met, then the life that is taken is no life, for in reality its lack will inflict no damage to nature.

- Beware that you kill no man even in the affirmation of the values you hold dearly; even in its justification and defense, for the act of murder embodies all forms of cultural illusions. When I talk of killing, my sense must thus be understood: it derives only from the element of productivity and human progress; that is, it must only be calculated in the sense of relevance after incarnation. If it achieves this cultural meaning, then it must be seen as being part of a larger nature; if it fails this primary test, then 'its' very force as a value, as a life-form is already denied by Its unproductiveness.

- I tell you this now because the whole of humanity is under the grip of a frightening self-inflicted cultural dilemma. I will try to make my meaning as simple as possible to you. Man lost his originality and sovereignty the moment he chooses God for himself as a protector and a Law-Giver. In doing this, he crosses the threshold of material nature wherein that sovereignty is reposed and enters the realm of cultural transcendence wherein the eternity and infinitude of God is legitimated. By so doing, he relinquishes his moral authority over himself and other men to God – this in itself is no cultural error, for the father-image and the father-figure, whether at the material or the transcendental plane, is a constant requirement – for the coherence of human community and culture.

- The cultural dilemma I speak of begins the moment man pretends that he is still a sovereign entity on earth, even after creating religious systems, shrines, altars, statues, rites and rituals through which he worships the God who has successfully snatched his sovereignty away from him. This contradiction is of a simple nature: man recognizes and accepts his subordinate relationship with God, yet man is forever playing God.

This is so, for God says to man: I am the one, the only and the last judge. None shall enter my kingdom unless he obeys all my laws, is guided by my laws and is judged by my laws. Man accepts this, prays over it, and yet keeps on pretending that these Laws exist only in their formal and not contentual sense.

- Here, we are concerned with only one Law: thou shall not kill. This is God's sovereign Law, for only 'Him' has the right to take a life when and as it pleases 'Him', for only 'Him' shall judge that life as he takes it.

God's judgement is never a collective one; it is a specific matter between an individual and God, so man believes. Man, in this situation, has no other invocation except to state his life as he lived it (this God already knows), and to be judged on the basis of that lived life, as a specific individual. Man cannot invoke circumstance, including self-defence, state duty, war situation, adverse condition, obligation, responsibility of office, legal enactments and statutes, in the justification of taking a life, for only God can so do without reservation, knowing fully well why he does so, and retaining the sole legitimate capacity to effectuate the consequences of such an act in eternity.

To take a life today on earth can only be justified under the context of material nature; no murderer, whatever the circumstance of murder, can legitimize his act before God, for his justification will run counter to the Law of God. He must render account of the murder he so committed as an individual, as an entity, with no support whatsoever from other entities who may well still be alive on earth, waiting for their translation into the realm of cultural transcendence before being subjected to their own judgement by God. God's judgement is never held in abeyance because all those involved in the chain of the committal of murder are not before 'His' presence, and even if such a judgement will come at the end of time, each and every individual must still render his own account of his life, without the possibility or opportunity of passing the buck to another person.

- What are the particulars of all these declarations, Njaa asked his disciples rhetorically. They are many. A judge or a jury sentences somebody to death because the Law demands such. The judge and the members of the jury have committed murder, yet they fail to recognize this. They are in fact satisfied with their state duty; they are protected by the Law. They are good Christians, Muslims, etc, and pray daily to God. It never occurs to them that their act is meaningless in the eyes of God, who must judge them on the basis of his Law, and not on the determinants of their earthly laws. After the sentencing, the hangman, a group of soldiers or a doctor who administers or operates a lethal injection machine carries out such a perfectly legitimate state duty. They too have committed murder in the eyes of God; they too shall be judged as murderers by God.
- The same applies to the president who prays in the church in the morning and later in the day orders that his fighters, bombers, missiles and rockets shall bombard another man's city, with human casualties. He too is a murderer, just as the fighter-pilot, the ground soldier who kills, and the rocket and missile launch men. They too shall stand before God and confess their act of murder ...
- I tell you this now. Mankind lives in a world of cultural delusion. No matter how elaborate his laws are on earth, he has lost his capacity of life-taking the moment he relinquished his autonomous existence and sovereignty to God. Be no part of such men, for the life that you may take should be non-productive lives, culturally speaking, and not lives that the state has decreed to be non-productive. Be no part of such cultural delusion for man believes in a cultural image in the form of a cultural force he calls God, who he claims has the final say in life, and yet who he defies at every turn, even when he pretends that he obeys him. Be no part of this cultural disease, for man searches in

vain for his lost sovereignty, inflicting damage on himself and other men, while at the same time claiming that everything is in God's hand.

Be no part of such men who will take a life because The Law says that they can, and, yet, who declare that what they do is in harmony with the wish of God. Man can only claim back his right to murder if he rejects the idea of cultural transcendence overseen by an omnipotent God. Until he does so, he remains a cultural idiot, who reaps where he did not sow and who gathers where he did not plant. Such men are idiots because they are pretenders here on earth and are doomed at the plane of cultural transcendence which they believe in.

When he finished saying all these things to them, Njaa departed from their midst and was seen no more or so they thought.

POSTSCRIPT

REINVENTING DECADENCE - THE NEW CULTURE OF CONTENTMENT:

A NOTE

The First and Second World Wars exhausted Europe; with that exhaustion came the collapse of its modern civilization in terms of autonomous values embodied in the freedom of cultural expression. Existentialism became the expression of the deepest sense of angst, ennui, and "shock" on the objective realization that **HITLERISM**, for instance, was not a marginal ideological imperative in European evolution but an integral statement of a deeply anchored historical process. America, which inherited the carcass of Europe and sensationalized its conquest of the old world via the Marshall plan, in fact, was already, at the mid-point of the century, "passing from barbarism to decadence". What it implanted into the soil of humanity was a mass counter-culture that denigrated the truest expression of cultural liberty.

Post-war European reconstruction became nothing but a caricature image of a deviant form of Pan-Americana, a process which later engulfed the whole of mankind and led to the present state of humanity's non-cultural existence. To understand this is to make a worthy distinction between cultural values incarnated by mass impulses and values generated by organic individuation in the arts, music, entertainment industry and the media. American ascendancy has led to the near irreversible retreat of individuated cultural values understood as an impetus driven by creative genius and to establish in its place a culture of titillation, ignorance, and imitativeness.

When, therefore, we speak of moving the centre of universal culture in favour of a multiplicity of cultural affirmations, as Ngugi wa Thiong'o does, our alarm should be directed at America, the one current constructer of the incoherence of universal cultural expressions. Take for instance, music. While before, operatic arias, symphonic orchestras and written music were the common properties of all classes even on their hierarchical demarcations; today, in spite of the popular appeal of Luciano Pavarotti, Placido Domingo, Jose Careras and other singers, composers and conductors, what is daily promoted as music is unmodulated noise that demeans the rhythm of nature. Even then, the mode and reach of "serious" music are presently dependent on the determinants of commerce which has become its life-force, its vitality, its viability, and even its legitimacy.

The lure of commerce, which of course has regimented living, welfare and prosperity to digital figures on stock market computer screens, lies behind the cultural insecurity of mankind. The inter-penetration of mercantilist ethic into all the layers of social intercourse necessitates a re-definition and revaluation of the core of existence in favour of mutilated media programming, hastily packaged news items and antiseptically "anchored" broadcasts. Commercial breaks have licked into all corners of existence as witnessed in the fidgeting and fitful glances at times by harassed programme presenters in the CNN for instance, who virtually shoo off their interview subjects irrespective of what is still meaningful that has yet to be said.

Watching the O. J. Simpson criminal trial – the high point of this disorder in terms of the collapse of the meaningfulness of culture – is one of the most debasing experiences anyone will go through. In it was the revelation of what America is today: psychically mangled, absurdly theatrical and downright sick. And because the show was hugely successful and enormously popular, in spite of the drama of life, pain and tragedy that was its substance, it means for me nothing but an ideal expression of a mentally stunted society whose monstrous resources implies – as a consequence of its universal significance – the eclipse of mankind's cultural renaissance in this century and beyond.

Maybe, I am so traditional in thought and imagination that I fail to recognize changes in culture, values, attitudes, systems of belief and structures of existence, with reference to the computer age, the information super-highway and the Internet, yet I remain convinced that the desperation that goes into the promotion of these values lack any serious pedagogical content, nor has it anything to do with true knowledge. This is because America still remains an ignorant society, and most Americans superstitious narcissists unwilling to learn the most basic realities beyond their shores.

The object of the new technological age is the demeaning and cheapening of knowledge and cultural values which are chopped off in bits in the World Wide Web and sold in uncouth goblets. It is an illustrationist, hand-me-down syndrome that deplores, resists and, in fact, abhors hard work, hard learning and hard intellect in favour – again – of commercialized mass shows and billions of information particles without coherence, structure and order.

Because I live in a different cultural atmosphere where access to information of a comparative nature is limited by a state system – a fledgling democratic order – I was somewhat startled by certain revelations regarding this matter in some contemporary American texts. I state this as an additional testimony for I have already declared my stand before this startling encounter. Readers only need to glance at Richard S. Wurman's *Information Anxiety,* David Sherk's *Dela – Surviving the Information Glut* and John

Naisbitt's *Megatrends* to appreciate this deep cultural crisis.

There is little doubt that the modern Western man is "drowning in information but starved of knowledge" and that no new, bold, innovative thought can emerge out of punching the computer keyboards – the current fad among American and Western scholars, intellectuals, academics and cultural thinkers – at the expense of the genius that flows from a well-held pen. The anxiety that is thus created by new information and communication technology is organically interlocked with the sense of inadequacy spawned by post-industrial societies that are inexorably bent on depersonalizing – and ultimately – robotizing social intercourse as the only legitimate form of cultural expression.

Cultural excesses are not indicative of the liberation of cultural values; they are rather symptomatic of a terrifying cultural disease. The chaos that attends licentiousness overdetermines, in a pre-conditioned manner, numerous moral assumptions that seek for social legitimacy. In America, for example, this is accommodated by the expansion of the bounds of morality, not in a progressive form, but as a purely necrophilic measure. With such an expansion of the horizons of legitimate cultural and moral values come shifts in attitudes, mutilation of language, and the over-professionalization of virtually all the fields of cognitive reasoning. Tendencies towards the re-definition, revaluation and reconnection of determinate and indeterminate values carry with them the burden of an already conferred legitimate status on all known deviant conducts. Sodomism and lesbianism, for instance, are interpreted as either alternative, accepted sexual practices, or as indications of individual sexual preference. Opposition to them is classified as a manifestation of a dangerous, quaint ultra-conservative Christian ethics that is anachronistic in an age of cultural and moral change.

What is thus clothed as the liberal state is nothing short of a state of unbelief. Liberalism in itself becomes a mere verbalization, not of contending alternative legitimate choices, but the constriction of choices under a permissive agenda. For when there is permissiveness in the context of the multiplicity of cultural expressions, there is a lack of choice in that all choices are real choices, no matter their impact on society and its inhabitants.

Societies must welcome change as an end-result of the inter-change of ideas and beliefs whose attribution is the production of values. The connectedness of evolutionary social dynamics which bears the stamp of classical heritage with new cultural utility will derive from a hidden structure and well-spring of meaning which a value system carries. Any system without an inherent structure must, of necessity, come to a startling historical dead-end. And any structure which carries with it a vacuous acceptance of unselective cultural particulars will suffer a double historical tragedy.

The trite comedy that the Western world has become is such that, one, its cultural assumptions presently lacks this hidden structure, and, two, when it exists exposes the injection of all forms and modes of permissible cultural contradictions. It is on this basis that such a civilization will ultimately collapse in spite of its high technocratic attainments.

The inculcation of cultural values which "time tries its teeth in vain", to quote again from Friedrich Nietzsche, has been the primary focus of all great literature in spite of its denial by Philistine leaderships in all sectors of life. These are the values that not only systematized the cognitive and perceptual capacities of mankind over the ages, but also helped to lay the foundation for the consolidation of humanity's transformation from beast to man. These are the shared experiences, presently spurned by the incarnators of anti-culture in which autonomous values are thoroughly disempowered, that characterize the works of Edward de Vere (Shakespeare), Bernard Shaw, Balzac, Goethe, Tolstoy, Dostoyevsky, Sholokhov, Pasternak, Achebe, Ngugi, Soyinka, Norman Mailer and others.

Contentment breeds complacency, ignorance,

superstition and contempt towards all creative and procreative endeavours. The fixation of consciousness on a non-instinctual belief in the limitless capacities of the artefacts of material nature is correspondingly matched by the unsubtle attenuation of life-forms which do not yield to this assumption. The absence of creativity is also seen in the vacuous life of the youth of post-industrial societies, stultified as they are with the certainties of artificial material and recreational pleasures; in the adult population by the absence of reflexive will and an inexorable descent into deviant conducts which are tolerated by liberalism and accommodated by the expansion of the legitimate zones of cultural attitudes.

In just the same way that Plato insisted on the banishment of poets from his ideal state in *The Republic* for the security of a complacent moral order; and George Sorrel saw in sports, war and entertainment the escapist elements of containment of mass pressures and passions in *Reflections On Violence*, latter-day ideologists of contentment have taken the issue to newer heights of affirmation. Francis Fukuyama, for instance, sees the possibility of the cessation of all productive intellectual thoughts in *The End of History and the Last Man* with the declared obsolescence of social and political philosophy in a neo-technocratic, de-ideologized, liberal democratic state.

In such a state, while better shoes, fabrics, computer chips and space stations will continue to be produced and built, mankind must cease in the art of the reproduction of new social, cultural and philosophical values.

Because sixties America never heeded the warning of Senator Fulbright in *The Arrogance of Power*, its narcissistic-globalist ideology of the period – right up to the seventies and early eighties – became a disaster. And because the perceptual genius of John Kenneth Galbraith who, in *The Affluent Society* saw the warning signs of America's permanent socio-economic decay, was ignored, that decay was to be later justified in his *The Culture of* **Contentment**.

Literature, which mirrors society, makes an eloquent statement about the contradiction between aspiration and the attainment of goals. Great literary works are not merely those which seek a reconnection with previous affirmations as T. S. Eliot indicated in "Tradition and Individual Talent" but those which stand at the threshold of the breakup of an old world and the beginning of an uncertain one. That is the force behind Dostoyevsky's *Crime* and *Punishment, The Devils and The Brothers Karamazov* (conflict between various persuasions of a moral order), and the strength that made Mikhail Sholokhov's *And Quiet Flows the Don* (the turmoil attendant on the birth of a new order), and Boris Pasternak's *Doctor Zhivago* (crisis of consciousness and moral excesses of an uncertain birth), two of the greatest novels ever to be written. Therein, too, reposes the power of Chinua Achebe's *Things Fall Apart* and *Arrow of God;* Ngugi wa Thiong'o's *A Grain of Wheat* and Gabriel Garcia Marquez's *One Hundred Years of Solitude*. These novels all resist the lure of complacency which is dictated by the over-determining will of a contented social system.

Of course, Nietzsche saw through the entire gamut of moral contentment when he declares in *Twilight of the Idols* that the liberal intimations which urge the dawning of a liberal state only remain liberal in the lack of its attainment; once established, a liberal order abandons its original impulses in the process of rationalization and systematization. This is to say that the self-containment of an evolved liberal state induces a sense of complacency and stiffening of consciousness that successfully challenges, and even contradicts, the fundamental perquisites of liberalism. And this is but a single example of the culture of contentment in the whole range of cultural discourse.

AFTERWORD

In the course of preparing the second edition of my works, and publishing for the first time the works that have remained in a manuscript form for years – a process which began in 2006 – I had cause to apply myself to a structured study of the pristine sources and historical evolution of Western philosophy. I also deepened my knowledge about the cultural and aesthetic theories of European, American, Asian and African thinkers that are vital for the substantial reconstruction of the scholarly works I wrote from the mid-1980s to the early 1990s. While this pursuit was coloured by an academic mindset, it nevertheless further exposed me to the profound philosophical and intellectual currents that were instinctually handled in the present work.

There are two ways of appreciating this 'radical' development. There is no doubt that the structure and content of *Autonomy of Values* would have differed considerably if I were to harness the philosophical knowledge available to me today in constructing its vision and laying out its central argument. A reading of the second edition of my *Revolutionary Aesthetics and the African Literary Process* will more than substantiate this claim. In preparing that edition, I spent the past seven or so years immersing myself in the sometimes bewildering universe of human imagination that is not only acute and intense but oftentimes presented in an impenetrable and obscurantist discursive mode.

Apart from my new engagement with Existentialist philosophy in which the location of metaphysics, epistemology and ontology appears most cogent, and considerable readings on positivism and antipositivism, empiricism, rationalism, historicism, idealism, materialism and phenomenology – all of which have direct and indirect bearing on my thoughts in the present effort – I was also relentless in my extraction of hidden truths in the minds whose thoughts have transformed the human realm as we presently know it. I had to revisit Kant, Hegel, Nietzsche, Marx and Kierkegaard, not just with an eye on their broad philosophic contributions to human knowledge but also with an alert ear to their formulations on aesthetics and cultural production. Again, from Georg Lukacs (whose History and Class Consciousness I never read when the draft of the work was completed) to the major Frankfurt School Critical Theorists across generational lines (Theodor Adorno, Max Horkheimer, Herbert Marcuse, Jurgen Habermas, Axel Honneth, Kompridis and Donald Kellner), I had so much to learn and absorb.

The same is equally true of my re-evaluation of the previous knowledge I had on the works of Christopher Caudwell, Walter Benjamin and Raymond Williams, not to speak about the passion I eventually developed for the philosophic, aesthetic and cultural thoughts of Louis Althusser, Lucien Goldmann, Pierre Marcherey, Fredric Jameson and Terry Eagleton. In the more central tradition of philosophy and psychology, I also found myself heavily engaged with the elaborate and complex constructs of Edmund Husserl, Martin Heidegger, Jean Paul Sartre, Jean Lacan, and in more contemporary terms, the discourses of Alain Badiou and Slovaj Zixek.

The French Poststructuralists and Postmodernists were equally within my searchlight's range. While previously I had very little information on them, today, I can possibly hold my own as a non-specialist would in the writings of Jacques Derrida, Michel Foucault, Jean François Lyotard,

Giles Deleuze and Jean Baudrillard. This is also true of my sustained interrogation of postcolonial theory and its canonization in the hands of Edward Said, Homi Bhabha, Gayatri Spivak, Aijaz Ahmad, E. San Juan and Ngugi wa Thiong'o. The list is quite extensive but what I have presented thus far is enough to locate the new bearings in my intellectual development and the multiform trajectories in my conception of philosophy, history, cultural studies and aesthetics as key agencies in human transformation.

Yes, while it is true that I am far better informed today than I was in 1998 when the original draft of the work was completed, meaning that I would have elected to construct my vision around this new knowledge in its current published form, I wisely, I hope, opted to retain and honour the integrity of not only the spirit of the initial effort but its instinctual aura as well. Like I did state in the introduction, the work was completed from start to finish, with minor exceptions, without my ever opening a book or a journal article to aid the cognitive and creative process. This is demonstrated not only in the absence of references to texts and other research materials in the body of the text (with the exception of the chapter on "Elysian Fields" and the elaborate quotations from the works of Fredrich Nietzsche in the chapter on "Masters of Consciousness"), but most importantly in the absence of bibliography at the end of the work.

I have already made the claim that my aim was to construct an intellectual piece and not to systematize academic knowledge. I maintain that a very wide gulf separates these two traditions of human knowledge. In conceiving and creating this sense of reality, I have elected to accept the judgement of readers and critics, no matter how harsh, than live with their praises and encomiums for a product which I cannot, in all honesty, claim as mine.

www.ingramcontent.com/pod-product-compliance
Lightning Source LLC
Chambersburg PA
CBHW020612300426
44113CB00007B/615